BUTTERCREAM FLOWERS

FOR ALL SEASONS

A year of floral cake
decorating projects
from the world's leading
buttercream artists

VALERI VALERIANO
AND CHRISTINA ONG

www.sewandso.co.uk

CONTENTS

INTRODUCTION

When we wrote and launched our book, *100 Buttercream Flowers* back in 2015, we didn't expect it to be such a huge success, and translated into ten different languages! The response to that first book specifically about piping flowers in buttercream has been absolutely overwhelming. Since its publication, flower piping has become a craze, so we thought it was high time to take this trend to the next level.

We are extremely happy to share with you our fourth book, *Buttercream Flowers for All Seasons*. We think you'll find that this is an excellent follow up to *100 Buttercream Flowers*; it will teach you to pipe more flowers and how to arrange them on your cakes. For those of you who do not make towering multi-tiered cakes, don't worry as we have also designed small versions and even cupcakes for you. Have we covered enough?!

Each of the cake projects will give you loads of ideas about how to arrange the floral elements, choose the right colours and all the other aspects to help you create your edible masterpieces. Our aim has been to maximise each cake 'canvas' to showcase as many flowers as possible, but we've also kept in mind that as the cake becomes smaller, it becomes more full. To be completely honest, we are not big fans of bouquet style cupcakes – the ones with a large number of blooms on each little cake. We've made a few extravagant cupcakes for this book, and they are without a doubt very pleasing to the eyes, but they can also mean too much buttercream for every bite. So if we were to make a dozen cupcakes, we'd probably just make between three and six 'bouquet style' ones and the rest would just be topped with a single flower to keep a good balance between cake and frosting. We would advise you to do this too.

We have carefully chosen beautiful flowers that will match the four seasons of the year: Spring, Summer, Autumn and Winter. Every project and flower is thoroughly explained in the easiest way possible so that anyone will be able to re-create it. We have included a lot of step-by-step photos to guide you, plus top tips aplenty.

We have tried to cover as many topics as we can to make sure that this book is a great and worthy addition to your cake-decorating book collection. We hope that it will inspire you and help you with your flower piping journey.

So beat your buttercream now and pick up your piping bag! If on your first go your piped rose looks rather more like a cabbage, just smile and say, 'what a *beautiful* cabbage I have made'! Then practise again.

Let's go #TeamBUTTERCREAM

Christina

Valeri

BUTTERCREAM BASICS

OUR BUTTERCREAM

Here we offer you the recipe that we have always used, tried and tested. This is our 'crusting' type of buttercream. As we travel and teach cake decorating in different parts of the world, during the summer season and in countries where it is hot and humid, we find that this is the best recipe for withstanding warm and damp conditions. To prove its stability, we actually covered and decorated a (dummy) cake with our buttercream and left it in direct sunlight at a temperature of about 38–44°C, for 2 to 3 hours. Yes, *we* may have melted while filming it, but the cake stood proud. The the main reasons this recipe remains our favourite are that it is very simple and quick to do, and heat-proof as well!

Another reason why we love this recipe is because of its 'crusting' quality, which means you can do so many different techniques to its surface. You can further smooth it to give a more professional look, just like the even finish you can achieve with fondant icing. Or you can partially blend in different colours before you smooth it, to give a cake a lovely marbled appearance, and there are so many other options too, as we'll explore in this book.

Basic buttercream recipe

The one thing you should remember is never over-beat your buttercream. If you do it will become grainy and the edges are likely to 'break' when you pipe your flowers and textures. When you over-beat, you incorporate lots of air in your buttercream, thus, the surface will have holes or 'air-pockets' when you spread it on the cake, making it hard to smooth. Remember that a hand-held mixer is not usually as powerful as a stand mixer, so if you are using a hand-held one, make sure you fold your mixture manually first until the ingredients are incorporated. This helps to avoid over-beating as well.

What is so good about our recipe is that a little less or more of a certain ingredient is fine. So if your buttercream is too stiff, add water or milk. If it is too thin, just add icing sugar (confectioners' sugar). Adjust it as you need to – all in moderation, of course. You may use your buttercream straight away to cover and decorate your cakes, but if you think it is too soft, we suggest you chill it in the fridge for about an hour, or touch the surface – if it is hard enough, take it out of the fridge.

YOU WILL NEED

- 225g (8oz) butter, room temperature

- 115g (4oz) medium soft vegetable fat (shortening) (Trex), at room temperature, OR 225g (8oz) of soft spreadable vegetable fat (shortening) (Crisco)

- 2–3 tsp vanilla essence, or your choice of flavouring

- 1 tbsp water or milk (omit if you live in a hot country or whenever the temperature is hot)

- 600g (1lb 5oz) icing sugar (confectioners' sugar) , sifted, if using medium soft vegetable fat (shortening) OR 750g (1lb 10oz) icing sugar (confectioners' sugar), sifted, if using soft spreadable vegetable fat (shortening)

- Mixer (hand-held or stand mixer)

- Mixing bowls

- Spatula

- Sieve (sifter/strainer)

- Measuring spoons

1. Beat the butter at medium speed until soft and pale (about 1 to 2 minutes). Some brands of butter are more yellow in colour, so to make it paler you can increase the beating time to about 2 to 5 minutes.

2. Add the vegetable fat (shortening) and beat for another 20 to 30 seconds or less. Make sure that it is well incorporated and that there are no lumps.

Important note: As soon as you add anything to the butter, you must limit your beating time to 20 to 30 seconds or even less.

3. Add vanilla essence, or your flavour of choice, and water or milk, then beat at medium speed for about 10 to 20 seconds until well incorporated.

4. Slowly add the sifted icing sugar (confectioners' sugar) and beat at medium speed for another 20 to 30 seconds or until everything is combined. You may want to fold the ingredients together manually before beating to avoid puffing clouds of sugar round your kitchen. Make sure you scrape the sides and bottom of your bowl, as well as the blade of your mixer, so you don't miss any lumps of icing sugar.

5. Lastly, after scraping the bowl, beat again for about 20 to 30 seconds and do not over-mix. This yields a perfect piping consistency of buttercream.

It is normal for the buttercream to have a somewhat 'grainy' texture when it is first made because you are merely combining the ingredients, and not cooking or dissolving the icing sugar (confectioners' sugar) to turn the mix into a liquid. To improve the texture, completely melt the vegetable fat (shortening) and leave it to cool before adding it to your beaten butter, then proceed as normal. After making the buttercream this way, it will look like it is curdled. Do not panic! This is also normal! Let it sit in your kitchen at room temperature for about 1 to 2 hours, to allow the powdered sugar to slightly dissolve into the vegetable fat (shortening) and butter mixture. Then chill the buttercream in the fridge for a few hours or until firm. Never beat your buttercream a second time with the mixer – just use a spatula and mix it manually, or 'massage' your piping bag to soften the buttercream.

ABOUT VEGETABLE FAT, AKA SHORTENING

This is a white solid fat made from vegetable oils, and it is usually flavourless or at least bland. You can find it in most supermarkets, next to the butter and margarines. It plays a very important role in our recipe as it helps make our buttercream stable, so you do not need to add too much icing sugar (confectioners' sugar) to make a stiff consistency, thus your frosting will have just the right sweetness. It also allows the surface of the decorated cake to 'crust' so it is not too sticky.

Different brands of vegetable fat (shortening) have different consistencies. If the consistency of your vegetable fat is hard, defrost it in the microwave first to soften and use 115g (4oz). If it is somewhat medium-soft to slightly hard, like Trex, use 115g (4oz) as well. If it is soft and very spreadable, like Crisco, you will have to double the amount to 225g (8oz).

Adding flavours

Flavoured buttercream will add character to your cake, and there are plenty of options to choose from: cocoa powder, fruit jam (jelly), peanut butter, squashed berries, or even green tea, to name a few. Just be mindful of consistency – make a batch of buttercream as described here, then add your flavouring; you can add a little water or icing sugar (confectioners' sugar) at the end to adjust the stiffness. Beware of squashed berries or fruit, which may have a high water content and can make your buttercream very runny. If this is the case, you can omit the water or vanilla essence to reduce the liquid content of the buttercream.

Coverage

If you make the basic buttercream recipe with the amounts given, one batch will yield approximately 1–1.1kg (2lb 7½oz) of buttercream. This will be enough to cover the top and the sides and to fill a 20cm (8in) round or square cake, depending on the design. This can be your guide to determine how much frosting you need to prepare. If you have any left over, just label it with the date you made it and store it in the fridge.

TOP BUTTERCREAM TIPS

• You may add milk, but if you do you can only keep your buttercream for two to four days, as milk has a shorter shelf-life. If you use water, you will be able to keep it for longer – about five to ten days.

• If you find the vegetable fat (shortening) does not incorporate well with the butter and you see lumps, or you think that the consistency is too hard, in future, beat the vegetable fat separately first before adding it to the recipe and then proceed as normal.

• If you need to make big batches of buttercream, just multiply all the ingredients according to how many batches you are making. You do not need to omit or add any of the ingredients as you double, triple, etc.

• If you find the buttercream a little sweet to your taste, either lessen the sweetness of your cake so it complements the icing, or take away about 60g (2¼oz) of icing sugar (confectioners' sugar) and replace it with cornflour (cornstarch). If you do this, make sure to blend and sift the sugar and cornflour well.

• Always keep your buttercream in sealed containers or re-sealable bags, so the surface will not dry out or crust.

• Occasionally you may need to freeze your buttercream. Just mark the date on the container, keep it sealed and use it within 30 days. When you are ready to use it again, follow the correct defrosting process – from freezer to the fridge, then fridge to room temperature.

Alternative buttercream recipes

At its simplest, as the name suggests, 'buttercream' is the result of creaming butter and powdered sugar. But you don't need to stop here as there is an amazing array of variations on basic buttercream. We have included another three recipes here and many more online at http://ideas.sewandso.co.uk/free-ebooks/ for you to try. They are all great for piping flowers but will have different stability. Not all of these are crusting types but they *are* all beautiful and yummy – we hope you enjoy!

ITALIAN MERINGUE BUTTERCREAM RECIPE

To make this light and fluffy buttercream, sugar and water are cooked to make a syrup while egg whites are beaten to soft peaks. The hot sugar syrup is added to the egg whites, which 'cooks' them, making them no longer raw. The meringue is whipped to stiff peaks until it's no longer warm. Room-temperature butter is added and mixed in until the frosting is light and smooth.

YOU WILL NEED

• 5 or 6 large egg whites

• 375g (13oz) granulated sugar

• 180ml (6¼fl oz) water

• 550g (1lb 4oz) unsalted butter, at room temperature

• 200g (7oz) solid vegetable fat (shortening), at room temperature (optional, makes it stable)

• 2 tbsp vanilla extract

• Pinch of salt and/or cream of tartar (optional)

1. In a large heavy-bottomed saucepan, mix half the sugar with the water over medium heat, and stir just until the sugar dissolves. Brush around the sides of the pan with a clean pastry brush dipped in water to dissolve any sugar crystals – you don't want the sugar to burn on the pan sides.

2. Attach a sugar thermometer to the side of the pan and continue boiling without stirring, until the sugar solution reaches 110°C (225°F)

3. Meanwhile, whisk the egg whites and remaining sugar in a stand mixer on low speed until the sugar is slightly dissolved. You can add a pinch of salt and/or cream of tartar for stability if you wish.

4. Once the egg whites are starting to become white in colour and forming stiff peaks, turn your mixer up to high and slowly pour the sugar syrup down the side of the bowl. Avoid splashing the syrup onto the whisk attachment so as not to make spun sugar.

5. Continue whipping the whites until the mixture has cooled down. The bottom of the bowl should feel barely warm.

6. Switch to the paddle attachment. Once the meringue is cool to touch, slowly add the butter/vegetable fat (shortening), which should be at room temperature, while beating at medium-high speed. Then slowly add the vanilla extract.

7. When the mixture is well blended and smooth, and when there are no remaining pieces of butter, you can stop or switch to the whisk attachment on low-medium speed to make the buttercream fluffy.

SWISS MERINGUE BUTTERCREAM RECIPE

This meringue buttercream is a slight variation on the Italian version, as the egg whites and sugar are heated over a pot of barely simmering water, which heats the egg whites to a temperature safe for consumption. It's just as delicious!

YOU WILL NEED

- 5 large egg whites
- 250g (9oz) granulated sugar
- 340g (11¾oz) unsalted butter, cubed and at room temperature
- 2 tsp vanilla
- ¼ tsp salt

1. Make a bain-marie (double boiler) by placing a bowl over a saucepan of simmering water, making sure the bowl doesn't touch the water.

2. Add the egg whites and sugar to the bowl, whisking constantly but gently, until temperature reaches 60°C (140°F), or until the sugar has completely dissolved and the egg whites are hot to touch.

3. Remove from the heat and pour into the bowl of a stand mixer with the whisk attachment and begin to whip until the meringue is thick, glossy, and the bottom of the bowl no longer feels warm – about 7 to 10 minutes.

4. Switch to the paddle attachment and, with mixer on low speed, add the butter cubes one at a time until incorporated. Continue beating until the mixture has a silky smooth texture. If the buttercream curdles, simply keep mixing and it will come back to smooth. If the buttercream is too thin and runny, refrigerate it for about 15 minutes before continuing to mix it with the paddle attachment until it comes together. Add the vanilla and salt, continuing to beat on low speed until well combined.

BEAN PASTE BUTTERCREAM (VEGAN OPTION)

This version is made with a puréed soft bean mixture, brought to simmer until the water is evaporated to create a thick paste that can be used to fill or decorate. It's a healthy alternative and also a vegan option.

YOU WILL NEED

- 500g (1lb 2oz) any white beans (or you can also try raw cashew)
- 250g (9oz) sugar
- ½ tsp salt
- 5 or 6 cups water

1. Rinse the white beans in cold water and soak until the beans are soft and double in size – for about 5 to 6 hours or overnight in the fridge.

2. Peel off the skin and drain the water.

3. Simmer the soaked white beans in 5 cups of water and add ½ tsp of salt over a high heat. Reduce the heat to medium and cook until completely soft. Skim off any foam that comes up to the surface. If necessary, add more water. When the water is at the level of the beans, remove the pan from the heat and cool to room temperature.

4. Use a blender to puree the bean mixture. This will yield a very runny consistency.

5. Heat the smooth white bean paste in a clean pan over medium heat. Add all the sugar and stir to mix. As the paste is heated and the sugar is dissolved, the paste will become loose. Stir with a wooden spoon so that steam bubbles out and the paste thickens again. Taste and adjust the sweetness by adding more sugar as you desire.

6. Turn off the heat. Let the mixture cool completely and keep it in an airtight container. If you will be using it within three days, keep it refrigerated, otherwise, keep it frozen. You can defrost the paste by moving it to the fridge the night before you need it.

COLOURING

Food colouring pastes or gels are ideal for colouring your buttercream as they won't affect its consistency. If you can only get hold of the powder type of colouring, make sure you dissolve it first with droplets of water to make it into a paste, as otherwise the powder granules will not dissolve properly into the thick consistency of your buttercream.

Because of the presence of butter in the recipe, buttercream has a tendency to have a yellowish tinge. This sometimes makes it difficult to achieve a very pale colour. For example, if you want to achieve a very light pastel blue, sometimes it will turn out pastel green instead. Therefore, if you want a light colour, tint your buttercream to white first, using a colourant such as Sugarflair Super White, before you add any other colour. Alternatively, add a hint of purple, which, because it is the opposite of yellow in the colour wheel, neutralises the yellowy hue. You do not need to do this if you are mixing dark colours.

Using colouring gels or pastes

This is the best method for mixing colours. Make sure you regulate the amount of gel or paste you apply as it is very easy to overdo it. For best results, prepare the buttercream at least 2 or 3 hours ahead of time to allow for any colour change as it is normal for buttercream to deepen in colour after a short while, especially with darker colours.

1. Use a toothpick (cocktail stick) and dip it into a pot of a concentrated colour gel or paste before smearing it directly into the surface of your bowl of buttercream. Never reuse the toothpick (A).

2. Use a spatula and smear the colour gel or paste across the surface, and scoop and fold the buttercream until no lumps of colour are present (B).

3. Repeatedly smear, scoop and fold the buttercream until the colour is completely even throughout (C).

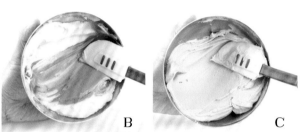

Using strongly tinted buttercream

We always suggest you mix your colours manually in a bowl so you have complete control of the results. It's often easier to gradually add buttercream in a strong shade of your desired colour to plain buttercream.

1. Tint a small amount of buttercream into a strong colour and gradually add small quantities into your plain buttercream (D).

2. Repeat the same mixing process (E).

3. Until you achieve even colour (F).

In cases where you need to mix huge amounts of tinted buttercream (like we do in our classes), you can gradually add your deep coloured buttercream into the plain buttercream and mix it under the stand mixer at the lowest speed for 10-20 seconds or until the colour is even. Be very careful not to over-beat it.

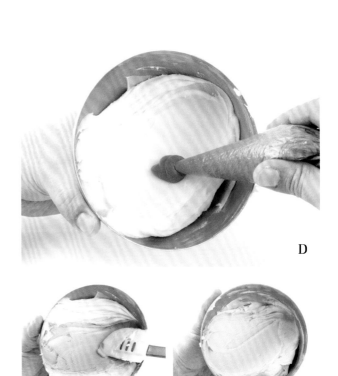

D

E   F

Adding white or black tinted buttercream

You will notice as you go through the projects in this book that we have sometimes added white to the already tinted buttercream (G and H), or start with white tinted buttercream before adding colour to it. This is not only for the obvious reason that it lightens the overall colour, but it somehow prevents the excessive heightening of the colour as well (I). However, we have also noticed that if you add a lot of white food colouring gel to your buttercream, the edges of the petals break easily when piping.

We also use this technique to tone down the intensity of a colour by adding black buttercream. This is especially helpful if the brand of food colouring gel that you are using yields very bright hues. If toning down a colour, we highly recommend making a concentrated black tinted buttercream and adding that, instead of adding the concentrated gel colour directly into the buttercream.

G

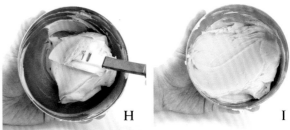

H   I

COLOURING TIPS

- If you think that you will be using a lot of food colouring paste to achieve a deep colour, do not add the water initially when making your buttercream, as this might result in it becoming too soft when the colouring is added.

- Make sure that your buttercream is at room temperature, or of soft consistency, for ease of mixing and incorporating the colours.

- It is typical for buttercream to heighten its colour after some time. Therefore, ideally prepare it 2 or 3 hours ahead of time.

Deep colours

Dark and deep colours are much harder to achieve than light shades. A true red or black or a strong brown can be tricky. Try the follow advice and you should have no trouble creating your desired colours.

BROWN

You can simply add cocoa powder to your buttercream to make a good brown. If you do, make sure to add a few droplets of water too, as adding a powdered ingredient such as cocoa powder will make your buttercream dryer and therefore stiffer. Alternatively, add some cocoa and some brown colouring gel or paste.

RED

Combine even amounts of any dark shade of pink (Sugarflair Claret, Fuchsia, etc) with orange and a strong red colouring gel or paste.

BLACK

Choose any dark colour as your base colour and use this to tint your buttercream. For example, turn your buttercream into dark blue, violet or brown first, then add the black colouring gel or paste.

EQUIPMENT

You don't need absolutely everything shown here to begin with, but having a reasonable range of nozzles and the tools for covering and smoothing your cakes is a good place to start.

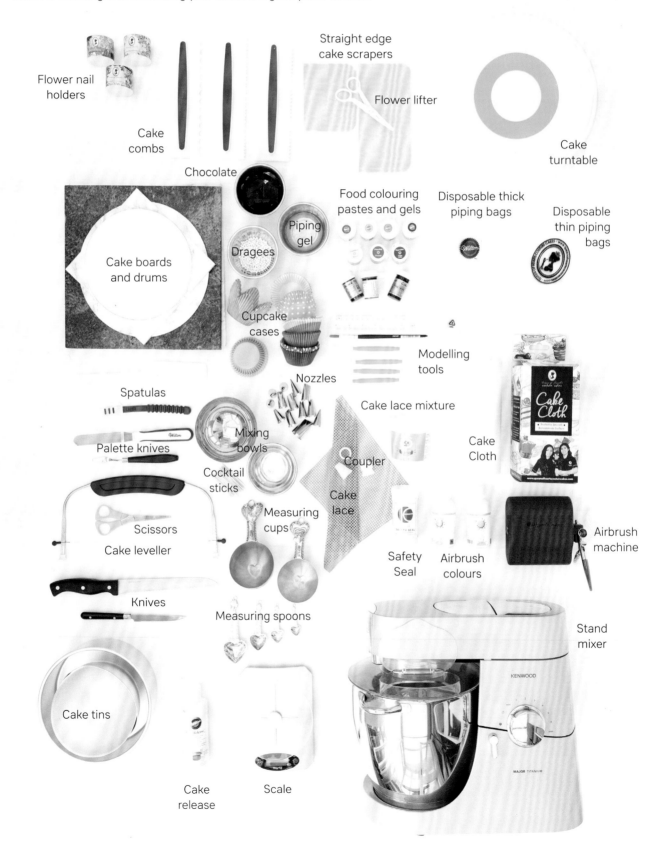

Flower nail holders

Cake combs

Chocolate

Straight edge cake scrapers

Flower lifter

Cake turntable

Cake boards and drums

Dragees

Piping gel

Food colouring pastes and gels

Disposable thick piping bags

Disposable thin piping bags

Cupcake cases

Modelling tools

Cake Cloth

Nozzles

Cake lace mixture

Spatulas

Palette knives

Mixing bowls

Cocktail sticks

Coupler

Cake lace

Scissors

Cake leveller

Measuring cups

Safety Seal

Airbrush colours

Airbrush machine

Knives

Measuring spoons

Stand mixer

Cake tins

Cake release

Scale

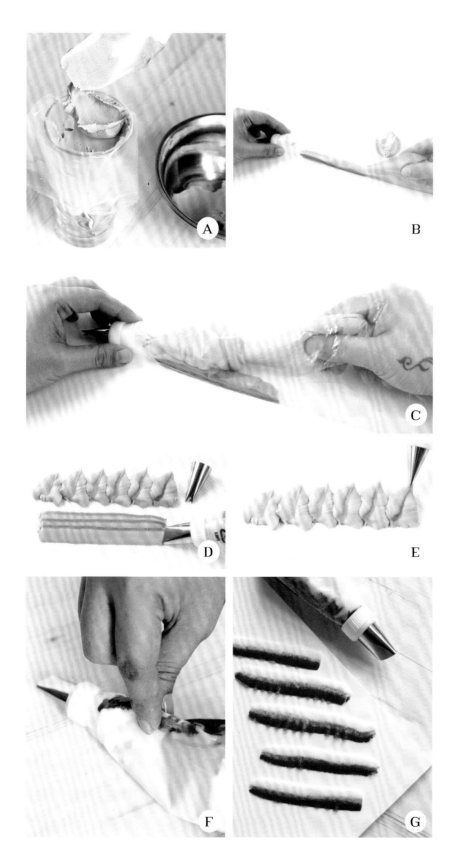

A

B

C

D

E

F

G

PIPING

Creating buttercream flowers is all about piping. Here are the techniques we have used to pipe the flowers and foliage in this book.

Filling a piping bag

SINGLE COLOUR

For a single colour, use a tall glass or vase to support your piping bag then scoop the buttercream into it (A).

TWO-TONE EFFECT

Place the 'stripe colour' buttercream in a plain piping bag, cut a small hole at the tip and pipe a straight line inside another piping bag. The thickness of this line will determine the broadness of the stripe (B). Then fill the bag with the main colour in the same way (C).

If you use a petal nozzle such as Wilton 101, 102, 103 or 104, the stripe will usually be where the narrow part of the nozzle is (D).

If using a leaf nozzle such as 352 or 366, the stripe should be aligned with one of the pointy tips (E).

BLENDED TWO-TONE EFFECT

To achieve a softer, more blended effect, repeat the same process as for the straight stripe effect, but randomly pinch the part of the bag where the stripe colour is to mix it with the dominant colour (F). Squeeze the piping bag until you're happy with the effect (G).

SMEARING

Choose the colour of buttercream you want to use as your additional colour and smear it unevenly on the sides of the piping bag using a palette knife (H). Avoid smearing any concentrated food colour as this could bleed into your buttercream, and it will be too much colour when you come to eat it. Fill the piping bag with your main colour by piping it in with a second bag (I). This technique was used to make the apples and lemons in this book (J).

MARBLED EFFECT

Prepare your chosen colours and place them in the same bowl (K). Blend them lightly with a spatula (L), then scoop the buttercream into your piping bag (M). Squeeze the piping bag until you get the right effect (N).

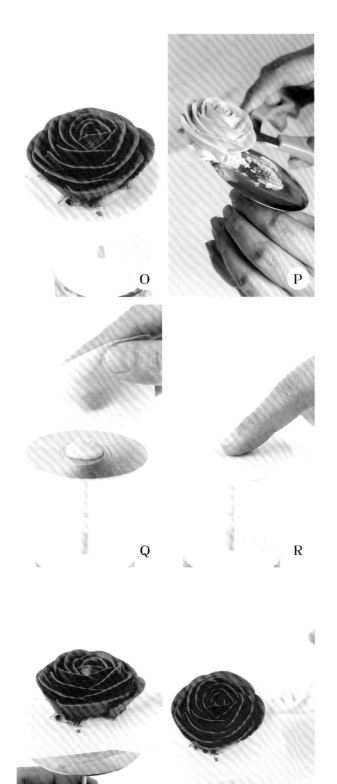

Piping flowers on a flower nail

Piping flowers on a flower nail is much simpler than piping the flowers directly on the surface of the cake because a flower nail is easier to turn and manipulate than the cake. By freezing the flowers you will make them much more easy to manipulate, arrange and secure onto the cake.

Do not hold your flower nail at the top near the plate as it will be difficult to turn. Instead, hold it near the bottom, between your fingers and your thumb. You should be able to easily and freely rotate it. It is also helpful to have a flower nail holder so that if you need to adjust your piping bag or do something else, you can rest the flower nail on the holder instead of sticking it in a styrofoam block or similar. A holder is also useful when you want to pipe small details onto a flower, like centres and spikes, when you can just place the nail on the holder (O).

LIFTING AND FREEZING

If you are lifting, you can pipe the flower directly onto the flower nail without any parchment paper under it, then use a flower nail lifter or scissors to 'cut' the flower, and lift and place it straight onto the surface of the cake while it is still fresh (P). This is ideal if your arrangement is on the top surface of your cake rather than on a corner or side. If you are doing this, remember that the flower is still soft and you can't put a lot of pressure on it when securing its placement, or you'll squash it!

If you are freezing your flower, make sure you use a small piece of parchment paper (Q) and stick it on the nail before you pipe the flower (R). After which, 'lift' to transfer the flower including the parchment paper (S) onto a tray (T), then freeze for no more than 10 to 15 minutes or until it is firm enough before arranging it on your cake. Do not freeze for too long as this can cause condensation or 'sweating' when you take the flower out of the freezer due to the sudden rise in temperature.

TIP

Alternatively, if you wish to place flowers on the side of your cake and think they might be too heavy, you can air-dry them at room temperature overnight, so the water content in the flowers partially evaporates leaving them lighter. Before you place them on the cake, freeze again for 5 to 15 minutes, or until hard enough to handle

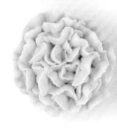

NOZZLES

Pictured below are just a selection of the piping nozzles you will need for the piping techniques and projects featured in this book.

Wilton petal
nozzle 102

Wilton petal
nozzle 103

Wilton petal
nozzle 104

Wilton petal
nozzle 124

Wilton petal
nozzle 97

Wilton petal
nozzle 116

Wilton petal
nozzle 150

Wilton
basketweave
nozzle 47

Wilton
chrysanthemum
nozzle 81

Wilton round
nozzle 5

Wilton round
nozzle 10

Wilton round
nozzle 12

Wilton star
nozzle 13

Wilton star
nozzle 14

Wilton leaf
nozzle 74

Wilton leaf
nozzle 65

Wilton leaf
nozzle 352

BUTTERCREAM BASICS

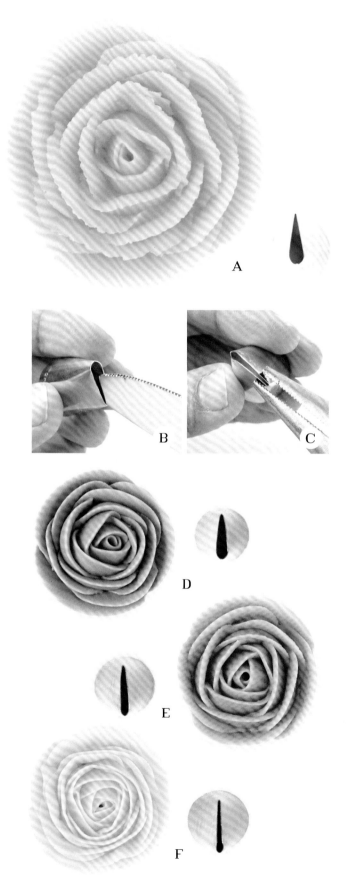

A

B

C

D

E

F

Manipulating piping nozzles

Piping nozzles are your main tools for the projects in this book, and as piping flowers becomes more and more popular people are trying to take inspiration from nature's beauty and are pushing the boundaries to create ever more realistic thin and crisp petals. Decorating supply companies have responded by innovating and improve different piping nozzles, and there is certainly a wide choice now. However, you may find that some of the nozzles are only available in some countries, and you won't be able to create those lovely petals because there are limited varieties where you are.

You might also find yourself looking for a particular type of nozzle because of the kind of buttercream you are using. If you use a thick type of buttercream, like our recipe, with a nozzle with a narrow opening you will sometimes find that the edges of your petals are inclined to break, and therefore you might need a slightly wider version of a nozzle, such as the standard shaped Wilton 104 shown here (A).

In addition to these frustrations, you will also find that different brands of piping nozzles have different shapes even though they have the same number. For example, the pointed tip of Ateco 104 is narrower or sometimes too closed compared to a Wilton 104. This can cause the edges of the petals to break.

Worry no more! You can achieve realistic petals using whatever type of buttercream recipe you wish to use with the help of two simple tools – pliers and a small knife – to manipulate your piping nozzles.

Using the blunt side of a small knife, insert it into the narrow end part of the nozzle and gently twist left and right to widen the opening (B).

To achieve crisp, thin and realistic petals, use the pliers and carefully pinch the nozzle opening to your desired size (C).

You can achieve different results by experimenting with manipulating the width of the nozzle opening, such as slightly opening the narrow end (D), slightly opening the narrow end and slightly closing the wider end (E), or completely narrowing the whole nozzle opening (F).

PIPING FLOWERS

This section contains all the techniques you need for piping the flowers required in the cake designs that follow. We have divided it by the main petal piping strokes: upright, pulled, simple, two-stroke and pressure piping/dots, and we've added special subsections of succulents (including cacti) and leaves. The flowers are listed at the beginning of each stroke, to make the instructions easier to find. Note that there are two type of dahlia, one that uses an 81 nozzle, and another that uses a 102 or 103 nozzle – make sure you are piping the right one. Also bear in mind that it is often easier to add the flower centres after you have attached the main body of the flower to your cake. You can press in the centre to make sure it adheres well without worrying about squashing the carefully piped flower centre.

UPRIGHT PETAL STROKE

This is the stroke used for piping roses, so we've started by explaining it via that very popular flower, although you can use it for a number of other blooms.

Used for: Rose, Pine cone, Anemone, Lisianthus, Ranunculus, Closed peony, Open peony, Kale, Carnation, Marigold, David Austin rose

Rose

Nozzles: 103, 104, 124 or 125

1. Pipe a sturdy medium-sized mound according to how big you want your rose to be (A).

2. Position the nozzle with the wide end touching the top centre of the mound, and slightly tilt it inwards to avoid piping too wide an opening at the tip of the cone-shaped centre of your rose (B).

3. To create the cone-shaped bud, squeeze the piping bag as you turn the flower nail until the two ends of your first piped petal meet and overlap (C).

4. Place nozzle in front of you while slightly tilted inwards towards the bud and continuously squeeze the piping bag as you pipe an upright curved petal in an arch-shape around the bud. Slightly push against the bud so there are no gaps in between and the petals stick together so it will not collapse (D).

5. Repeat the same process and make sure each petal overlaps from the previous one, a little past the middle. Ideally make two or three petals like this (E).

6. After a few petals, hold the nozzle straight, so the opening is vertical, and pipe four to five slightly longer and higher arched upright curved petals (F).

7. When piping the last few petals, tilt the nozzle slightly outwards and make the arches longer instead of higher. Pipe about four to five petals or more, depending on how big you want the rose to be (G).

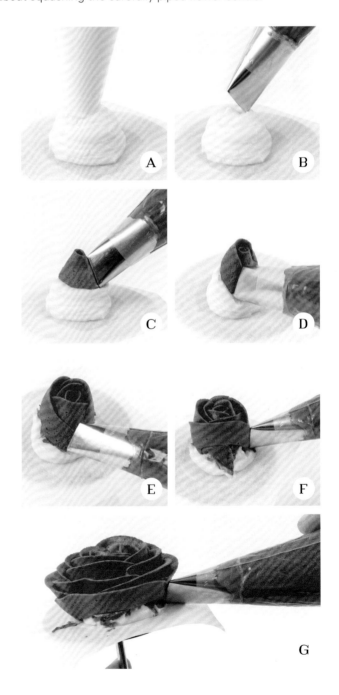

Pine cone

Nozzles: 102 or 103

1. Repeat steps 1–4 as for the rose, but keep all the petals upright instead of tilted (H).

2. For the succeeding layers of petals, continue piping with same size petals throughout, making sure that the petals slightly overlap from the previous layer (I).

3. Continue piping the layers of petals lower down your foundation blob than you would for a rose (J).

Anemone or Lisianthus

Nozzles: 103 or 104

1. Pipe a small round flat base as a foundation blob (K).

2. Pipe the centre for lisianthus with spikes, using a piping bag with a small hole at the tip (although these can be added after the flowers are attached to the cake). Or pipe the anemone with a typically black flat round centre surrounded with spikes (L).

3. For either flower, position the nozzle upright at the edge of the centre and pipe upright petals making sure that each petal overlaps from the previous one (M).

4. The petals should become longer, slightly higher and slightly tilted outwards as the flower gets bigger (N).

Ranunculus

Nozzles: 104, 124 or 125

1. Pipe a small round blob for the centre (A).

2. Tilt your nozzle towards the centre and pipe a continuous upright petal all the way around (B).

3. Repeat the same process and pipe two to four layers of continuous upright petals (C).

4. Pipe more layers of simple upright petals that are slightly tilted inwards. You can change the colour of the buttercream as you continue to add petals. As the flower becomes bigger, the angle of the nozzle can also gradually tilt outwards (D).

Closed peony

Nozzles: 104, 124, 125, 97L, 116L or 61

1. Pipe the centre in the same way as for a ranunculus. If using 97L and 61 nozzles, start piping the petals from the back of the flower, then towards you (E).

2. Repeat steps 3–4 as for the ranunculus (F).

3. You can switch to a larger 104, 124 or 116L nozzle for the last few petals, to make sure the petals reach from the base of the flower to the top and don't leave big gaps on the bottom (G).

Open peony

Nozzles: 104, 124, 125, 97L, 116L or 61

1. Pipe centre spikes as for a lisianthus, then start piping small and short upright petals (H).

2. Continue piping petals in the same way as for a rose, but intentionally make some petals ruffled by giving your hand a slight up and down movement as you pipe. If using a 97L (or 116L) nozzle, you will find that your petals typically come out ruffled (I).

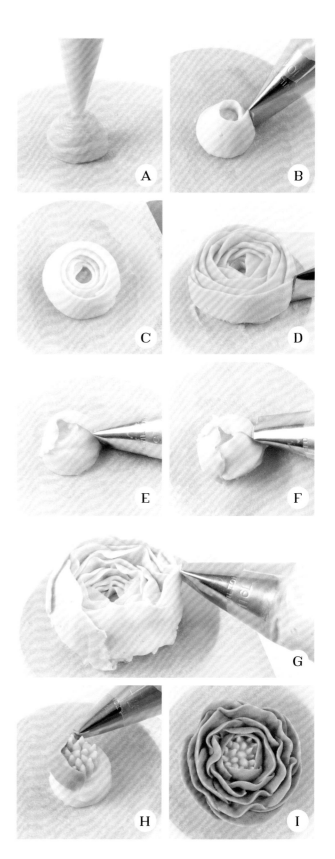

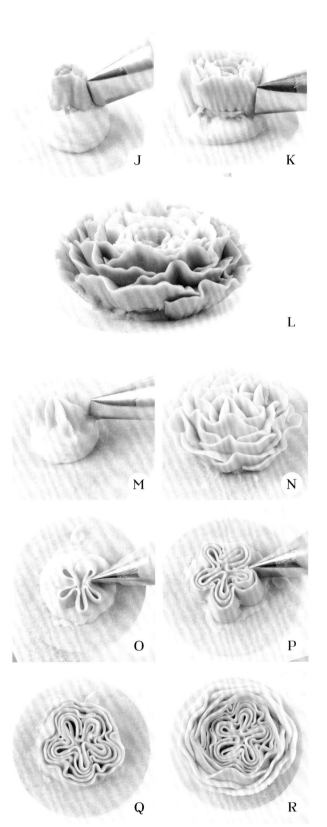

Kale

Nozzles: 103, 104, 124 or 125

1. Pipe kale using the same technique as for a rose but make each petal very ruffled (J).

2. You can do this by moving your hand with very rigid up and down motion (K).

3. You can also change the colours of the buttercream for the layers of petals as the kale becomes bigger (L).

Carnation or Marigold

Nozzles: 103, 104, 124 or 125

1. Pipe as kale, but make the petals less ruffled. You can do this by moving your hand just slightly up and down as you pipe. The centres for both the carnation and marigold are composed of short upright petals (see Kale) concentrated on the centre (M).

2. Continue piping layers of slightly ruffled petals (N).

David Austin rose

Nozzles: 103, 104, 124 or 125

1. It works really well if you use two-tone buttercream in your piping bag for this rose (see Buttercream Basics). Just rotate the nozzle to change the shade as you need. To create the centre, continuously pipe a small, rounded star-like centre composed of little loops of upright petals (O).

2. Pipe three to five more of the same petals following the same shape. Tuck them together so they look tightly packed (P).

3. Continue piping two or three rounds of low upright petals while making sure you fill any gaps (Q).

4. Carry on with upright petals around the centre, depending on how big you want the flower to be (R).

PULLED PETAL STROKE

Using a leaf nozzle such as Wilton 352 you can not only create simple foliage, ideal for filling gaps between flowers, but also make large petalled flowers. The technique is the same even if you use a different nozzle: pulling outwards until the leaf or petal is the desired length, hence 'pulled petal' stroke. Note that this section includes the kind of dahlia you pipe with a chrysanthemum nozzle 81, but not the other slightly more open kind.

Used for: Sunflower, Clematis, Poinsettia, Dahlia 81, Chrysanthemum, Gerbera daisy, Pulled blossom, Tulip, Leaves

1. Hold the piping bag at a 20–30 degree angle with one of the pointed ends of the nozzle touching the surface and the other pointing upwards (A).

2. Squeeze the piping bag with constant pressure until the buttercream creates a wide base (B).

3. Gradually pull the piping bag while continuously squeezing but gradually releasing pressure as you reach the desired length of your petal or leaf (C).

4. Once you reach the desired length, stop squeezing the bag and pull the nozzle abruptly (D).

Sunflower

Nozzle: 352

Pipe two or three concentric rows of pulled petals. Add dots in the centre using a piping bag with a small hole at the tip. The dots can be added after the flower is attached to the cake if you are pre-piping it (E).

Clematis

Nozzle: 352

Make one row of medium-sized petals, and add spikes in the centre, as shown. The spikes can be added after the flower is attached to the cake if pre-piping (F).

Poinsettia

Nozzle: 352

Use more pressure to create bigger, longer petals. Make five to seven in your first layer, four or five in the second, and pipe five to seven big dots in the centre using a bag with a medium hole at the tip. The dots can be added after the flower is attached to the cake if pre-piping (G).

Dahlia 81

Nozzle: 81

1. Start with a big round mound of plain buttercream to create the main shape and size of your flower (H).

2. Starting from the bottom, pipe layers of even-sized short petals. Hold the nozzle with curved part down and the opening touching the mound. Give the piping bag a squeeze as you pull, but quickly release the pressure (I).

3. Carry on piping more layers of petals while making sure you don't leave any gaps. You can either create the whole flower with these petals or leave a small gap to pipe spikes on the top centre (J).

Chrysanthemum

Nozzle: 81

1. Pipe longer petals than for a dahlia, starting from the outer layer and holding the piping bag at about a 20–30 degree angle (K).

2. Succeeding layers should gradually increase in the steepness of the angle. Pipe two or three layers of petals. Try to pipe the petals in between the previous layers of petals (L).

3. Pipe spikes in the centre with a piping bag with a hole at the tip (after the flower is added to your cake if pre-piping). When the surface has crusted, you can smooth the edges and tips of each petal by gently tapping them with your finger (M).

Gerbera daisy

Nozzle: 81

1. Pipe two layers of long pulled petals at a low angle of about 10 degrees, or almost flat (N).

2. Cut the tip of a plain piping bag into a small 'v' shape and pipe a few short rounds of spikes (O). We've shown some spikes piped on a board so you can see the desired shape clearly (P).

3. Finish the centre with yellow spikes using a piping bag with a small hole at the tip, and add black spikes right in the centre. The centre can be added after you have attached the daisy to your cake, if pre-piping (Q).

Pulled blossom

Nozzles: 101, 102 or 103

1. Use a small petal nozzle like 101, 102, 103 and hold the nozzle either sideways or with the opening facing the surface. Squeeze the piping bag as you gradually pull, then release pressure when you reach the desired length (A).

2. Repeat the same principle for the rest of the petals, then pipe the centre (B).

Tulip

Nozzles: 101, 102, 103 or 104

1. Pipe a narrow and slightly elongated blob, then pipe spikes for the centre using a piping bag with a small hole at the tip (C).

2. Hold the piping bag straight up with the opening of the nozzle flat onto the surface. Squeeze the piping bag as you pull either vertically upwards or with a slight curve inwards. Release pressure when you reach the desired length of each petal. Each succeeding petal should slightly overlap the previous one (D).

3. Repeat the same process for more layers of petals. Make sure there are no gaps in between them (E).

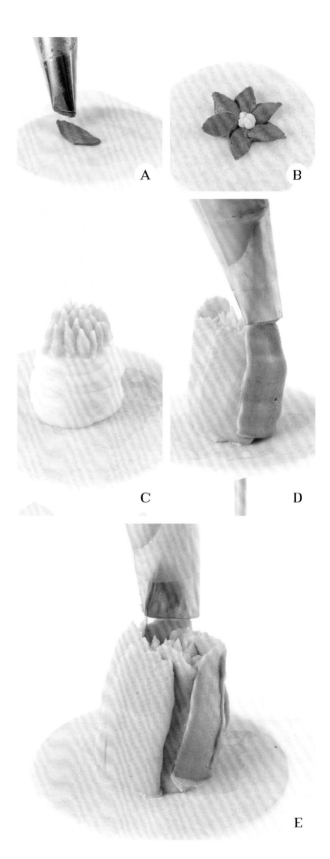

A

B

C

D

E

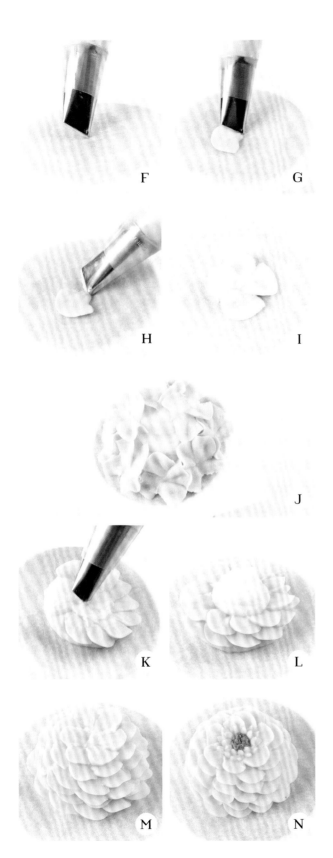

SIMPLE PETAL STROKE

A straightforward and versatile stroke, use simple petals to create a wide range of flowers.

Used for: Hydrangea, Delphinium, Dahlia 102-103, Magnolia, Freesia, Sweet pea, Camellia

1. Position the nozzle at a 20–30 degree angle with the wide end of the nozzle touching the surface and the narrow end pointing outwards. The narrow end of the nozzle should be in a 12 o'clock position (F).

2. Give the piping bag a good squeeze without moving or turning your hands or your piping bag. The wide end of the nozzle should remain in the same position (G).

3. Gently pull the piping bag down or towards you so that the petal has a clean edge. Release the pressure when the buttercream creates a simple petal shape (H).

Hydrangea or Delphinium

Nozzles: 102 or 103

1. For each of the small flowers, join four small simple petals together around a common central point. Pipe a dot in the centre, as shown on a flat surface here (I).

2. For a hydrangea 'head', pipe a big round mound then pipe small flowers that overlap slightly with each other. Using two-tone buttercream works well for this flower (see Buttercream Basics). To create delphiniums, pipe the small flowers in more of a row, with a few clustered at the base. Pipe a dot in the centre of each flower (J).

Dahlia 102-103

Nozzles: 102 or 103

1. Pipe a flat round base mound according to how big you want the flower to be, then pipe your first layer of simple petals (K).

2. Pipe a second layer of petals that make a slightly wider circle than the first layer to begin to create a ball shape. Before progressing to the next layer, fill the centre with a little blob (L).

3. Repeat the process for the next layers of petals to keep the ball shape (M).

4. Leave a space on the top for the centre spikes and dots, which can be added with a piping bag with a small hole at the tip after the flower has been attached to your cake, if pre-piping (N).

Magnolia

Nozzles: 104, 124 or 125

1. Pipe a wide petal by holding your bag at a 20-30 degree angle and continuously squeezing as you move your hand to create a big, wide fan-shaped petal (A).

2. Make about five or six petals in the first couple of layers (B).

3. Add four or five petals to make the second layer, then pipe spikes and dots in the centre using a piping bag with a small hole at the tip (C).

Freesia

Nozzles: 102, 103 or 104

1. Pipe two simple petals that are side by side (D).

2. Pipe one or two more petals on top to complete each flower (E).

3. Repeat the process to create clusters of flowers, then pipe short spikes in the centre of each using a piping bag with a small hole at the tip (F).

Sweet pea

Nozzles: 102, 103 or 104

1. Pipe two simple petals side by side (G).

2. Then pipe two upright petals (see Freesia) on the base of the first petals, in the centre (H).

Camellia

Nozzles: 102, 103 or 104

1. Pipe a circular layer of simple petals close to each other (I).

2. Repeat the same process to create one or two more layers, making sure each layer makes a smaller circle within the one below, then pipe spikes in the centre using a piping bag with a small hole at the tip. The spikes cane be added after the flower is attached to the cake, if pre-piping (J).

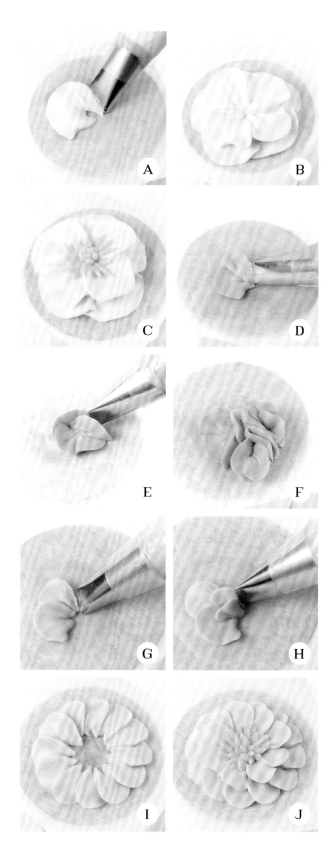

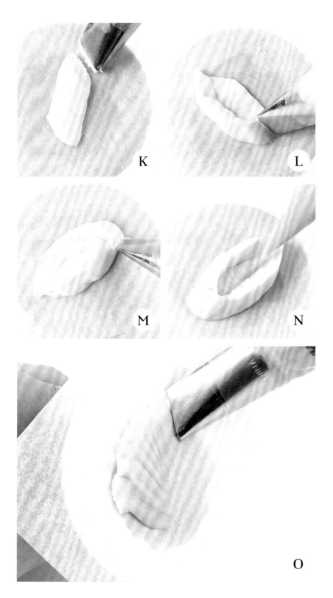

TWO-STROKE PETAL

As the name implies, this is an up-and-back-again piping stroke that can create flat foliage, such as photinia leaves, or slipper-like flowers, such as calla lilies, if the second part of the stroke is more upright.

Used for: Calla lily, Foliage

Calla lily

Nozzles: 104, 124 or 125

1. Pipe a flat pulled petal (see Pulled Blossom) making sure that the tip of the petal is pointy. This will be the length of your flower (K).

2. Position the opening of the nozzle flat on the surface with the narrow end pointing outwards. Pipe an upright petal as you continuously squeeze the piping bag while dragging it down to the base of the flower, and fold towards the centre (L).

3. Repeat the same process on the right (M).

4. Pipe the centre using pressure piping (see Pressure Piping), gradually releasing the pressure towards the tip (N).

Foliage

Nozzles: 104, 124 or 125

1. Start piping one side of the petal by positioning your nozzle facing left, flat on the surface. Squeeze piping bag with constant and even pressure either in a jiggling motion or just drag smoothly to the tip of the petal (O).

2. Repeat the same process on the right side but starting from the tip going back to the base (P).

OTHER PETAL STROKES

The following flowers require a variation on the piping strokes already described.

Used for: Dogwood flower, Peach ruffle flower, Scabious flower, Scabious pods

Dogwood flower – heart-shaped petals

Nozzles: 103 or 104

1. Pipe a heart-shaped petal by holding the piping bag flat to the surface and piping a short petal with a curve to the right (left if you are left-handed) at the top to make half the heart; release the pressure then pipe the other half of the petal as a mirror image of the first (A).

2. Pipe four petals that are touching at the base (B).

3. Using piping bags with a small hole at the tip, pipe dots in the centre and highlight the bract with a light brown or green line (C).

Peach ruffle flower

Nozzles: 103 or 104

1. Pipe simple petals, using the same method as for magnolia (see Simple Petal Stroke), but create a ruffled effect by wiggling the bag as you pipe (D).

2. Create the bottom layer with about five petals (E).

3. Add a second layer with another five, slightly smaller, petals (F).

4. Complete the centre with tiny dots (G).

Scabious flower – ruffle petals

Nozzles: 103 or 104 and 81

1. Make each petal by piping up to the top of the petal and down to the base again. Create alternating longer and shorter petals as you complete a layer (H).

2. Pipe a second layer of petals on top of the first and fill the centre (I).

3. Pipe the centre in a similar way to the dahlia, but using a Wilton chrysanthemum nozzle 81 to make the outer ring, then adding dots in the very centre (J).

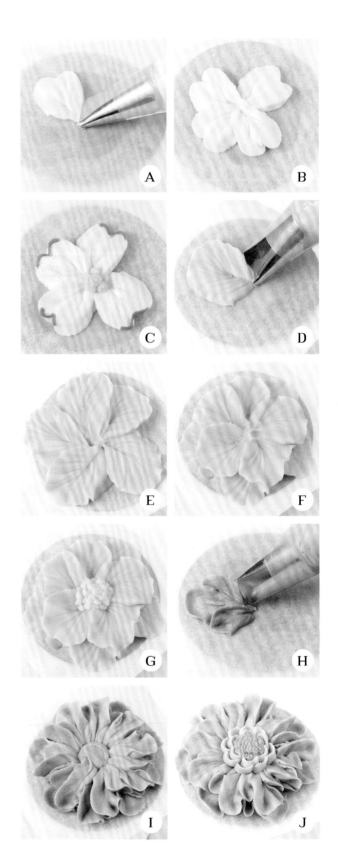

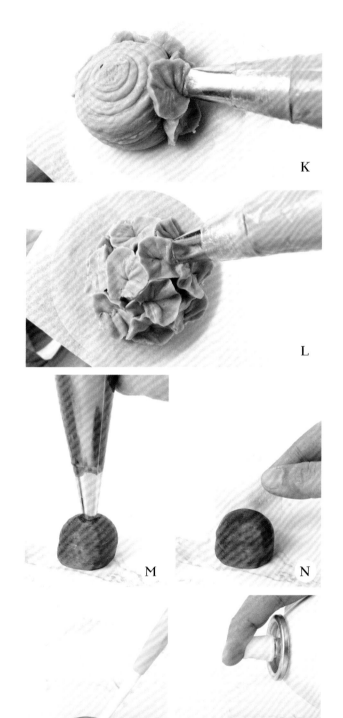

K

L

M

N

O

P

Scabious pods – multiple ruffles

Nozzles: 101s or 101

1. Pipe a big round mound of buttercream as the base. Starting at the bottom, pipe a small ruffle flower. To do this you can either continuously pipe a small, flat, circular ruffle petal as one whole flower or join two half-ruffle petals (K).

2. Carry on piping more of these flowers until the whole ball is covered (L).

PRESSURE PIPING

There is really nothing complex about this technique – you just adjust the pressure you use as you squeeze your piping bag depending on what you want the output to be. Less pressure will yield a dot or a small flower. A lot of pressure will yield a ball, mound or a big petal. For different shapes you just continuously squeeze your piping bag as you slowly move your hand in the direction necessary to create that shape. You build up the buttercream into your desired shape using the pressure you put into squeezing your piping bag. To create raspberries and blackberries, pipe a round foundation blob, then cover it with small dots in the correct colour for that fruit. Some of the other larger flower and fruit elements are described below.

Used for: Baby's breath, Raspberries, Blackberries, Brunia berries, Filler flowers, Billy ball flower, Thistle centre, Poppy pod, Apple, Lemon, Acorn, Cotton flower

Apple

Nozzle: 12

1. Start by using the smearing technique when you fill your piping bag (see Buttercream Basics). Hold the nozzle vertically with the opening flat onto the surface and slowly build up the shape using pressure piping (M).

2. Let it crust for 5 to 10 minutes and use a small piece of Cake Cloth to smooth the surface by gently patting it. You can also improve the shape of the apple to make it more realistic at this point (N).

3. Use a pointy modelling tool to make creases in the top part of the apple (O).

4. When you are happy with the shape, use a spray glaze like DinkyDoodle Shell & Shine to give the apple a nice gloss (P).

Lemon

Nozzle: 12

1. Repeat step 1 for the apple but aim for an oval shape base rather than wide and round (A).

2. When at the top, squeeze with very gentle pressure to create the tip of the lemon (B).

3. Leave to crust for 5 to 10 minutes and use a rounded flat modelling tool to flatten the tip of the lemon (C).

4. Use an old paint brush and lightly press onto the surface to create a textured look (D).

Acorn

Nozzle: 8 or 10, or none, and 13

1. Use a plain piping bag with a medium hole at the tip or a Wilton round nozzle 8 or 10, and create the body with pressure piping, reducing your pressure towards the top to create a pointy tip. Then freeze for 5 to 10 minutes (E).

2. Turn the acorn onto its side after removing it from the freezer, then use a Wilton star nozzle 13 to create the shell by continuously piping a ruffled swirl starting from the edge of the acorn to the base. Give the piping bag a good squeeze to create a cupped shape for the top (F).

Cotton flower

Nozzle: 10 or 12, or none

1. Use the pressure piping technique to pipe four to five medium-sized 'cotton balls' that are close together (G).

2. Pipe the details with brown buttercream in a piping bag with a hole at the tip (H).

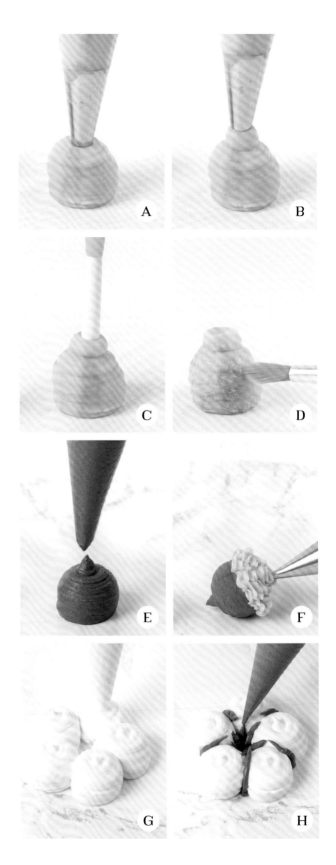

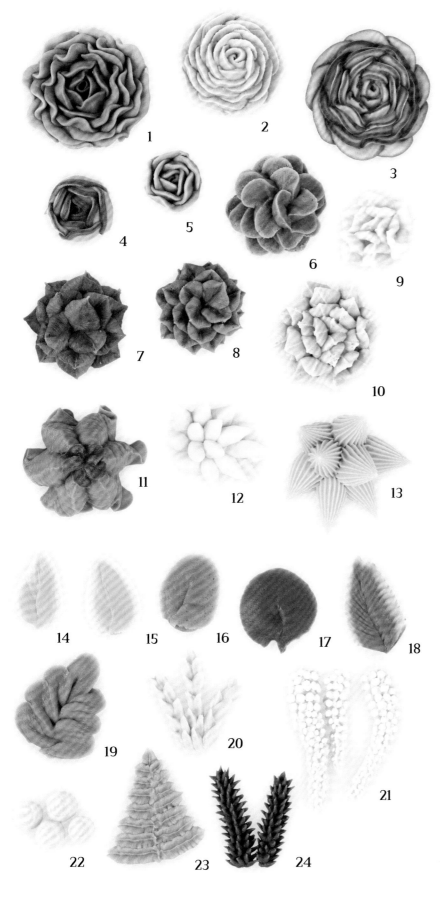

SUCCULENTS

1, 2, 3, 4 and 5 – use the upright petal stroke technique (see Rose) with a Wilton 150 nozzle.

6 – use the simple petal stroke technique (see Camellia) with a Wilton 103 nozzle.

7, 8, 9 and 10 – use the pulled petal stroke technique (see Sunflower) and a Wilton 352 nozzle.

11 – use the pressure piping technique and a Wilton 1M nozzle. Add a blossom using a Wilton 102 nozzle and the simple petal stroke technique.

12 and 13 – use the pulled petal/leaf stroke. Use a plain piping bag for 12, and Wilton 18 nozzle for 13.

LEAVES

14, 15, 16, 17 and 18 – use the two-stroke petal technique (see Foliage) and a Wilton 102, 103, 104 or 124 nozzle, giving the leaves a pointed or rounded tip.

19 – use the simple petal stroke technique and a Wilton 102, 103 or 104 nozzle.

20 – use the pulled petal stroke technique and a Wilton 102, 103 or 104 nozzle.

21 – pipe the main shape using the pressure piping technique and a Wilton 13, 14, 16, or 18 nozzle, then cover it with dots using a piping bag with a small hole at the tip.

22 – pipe a small mound of the main colour, then insert a piping bag with a Wilton 1 or 2 nozzle and squeeze until the pink surfaces.

23 – pipe long leaves as shown, using a Wilton 65 nozzle.

24 – pipe lines, then cover them with short spikes using a piping bag with a small hole at the tip.

CAKE BASICS

CAKE RECIPES

Madeira cake

This recipe makes a nice dense sponge cake that is easy to carve and stack – and it's absolutely delicious! The quantities given will make a 20cm (8in) round cake. If you are making Our Naked Cake, add a little green food colouring to each of your cakes, increasing the amount incrementally from a pale green to a dark one.

YOU WILL NEED

- 250g (9oz) unsalted butter
- 250g (9oz) caster (superfine) sugar
- 250g (9oz) self-raising (-rising) flour
- 125g (4½oz) plain (all-purpose) flour
- 5 large eggs
- ⅛ tsp salt
- 2–3 tbsp milk

1. Pre-heat the oven to 160°C (325°F). Grease your cake tin, line the base with parchment paper and grease the paper.

2. Cream the butter and sugar in a large bowl until light, fluffy and pale. Sift the flours together in a separate bowl.

3. Beat in the eggs, one at a time, beating the mixture well between each one and adding a tablespoon of flour with the last egg to prevent the mixture curdling.

4. Gently fold in the flour and salt, with enough milk to give a mixture that falls slowly from the spoon.

5. Transfer to the lined cake tin and bake for 1 to 1½ hours. When the cake is ready, it will be well risen, firm to the touch and a skewer inserted into the centre will come out clean.

6. Turn it out onto a wire rack to cool completely.

Chocolate mud cake

This recipe makes a dense cake that behaves well when you use it for stacking and carving.

YOU WILL NEED

- 250g (9oz) salted butter
- 250g (9oz) dark or milk chocolate (chopped or broken)
- 8tsp instant coffee
- 180ml (6¼fl oz) water
- 150g (5½oz) self-raising (-rising) flour
- 150g (5½oz) plain (all-purpose) flour
- 60g (2¼oz) cocoa powder (unsweetened is best)
- ½ tsp bicarbonate of soda (baking soda)
- 500g (1lb 2oz) caster (superfine) sugar
- 5 eggs, lightly beaten
- 70g (2½oz) vegetable oil
- 125ml (4fl oz) buttermilk (to make: add 1 tbsp lemon juice or white vinegar to one cup of milk and let it sit for 5–10 minutes)

1. Pre-heat your oven to 160°C (325°F), then grease and line your baking tins.

2. Combine the butter, water and coffee in a saucepan over heat until they come to a slow boil. Turn off the heat and pour in the chocolate, stirring until it is completely melted. Set aside.

3. Sift the flours, cocoa powder, sugar and bicarbonate of soda (baking soda) together in a large bowl, and make a well in the centre.

4. Pour in the eggs, buttermilk, oil and chocolate mixture and stir vigorously with a wooden spoon until there are no lumps.

5. Pour into your prepared tins and bake for approx 45 minutes for a 15cm (6in) cake or 1¼ hours for a 20cm (8in) cake. Remove the cake from the oven when a skewer inserted in the middle comes out clean.

6. Allow the cakes to cool completely in the tins before removing them.

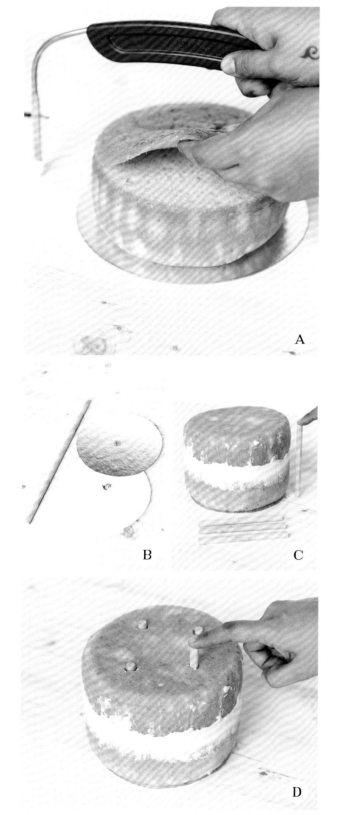

A

B

C

D

STACKING AND DOWELLING

As your cake becomes taller you must add some structure to support it, to make it sturdy so that it will not collapse. You will need plastic or wooden dowels (or even large plastic straws) inserted properly into the lower layers of the cake, to bear the weight of the cake above and to make sure that each layer does not get squashed and collapse.

Our rule of thumb is that you can stack up to three cake sponges without needing to dowel, but as soon as you need to increase the height beyond this, make sure you support the structure with dowels.

YOU WILL NEED

- Four cake sponges of your chosen size
- Three 1–2mm (1/16in) thin cake boards (fairly sturdy but still possible to cut – not cake cards)
- Cake drum
- Cake leveller or serrated knife
- Plastic or wooden dowels
- Wire cutters or heavy-duty scissors
- Pencil or pen
- Glue

1. Use a cake leveller or serrated knife to trim the top surface of all the cake sponges to make them level (A).

2. Cut the thin boards about 5–10mm (1/4– 1/2in) bigger than the size of the cake, or slightly bigger if you want the buttercream to be thicker. (Usually you can use the bottom of the baking tin that you used to bake the cakes as your guide.) Glue two thin boards together back to back (with the silver-coating outwards) and insert a dowel through the middle to create a hole. Keep turning the dowel around to make the hole slightly bigger so that it is easier to insert later (B).

3. Place the first two cake sponges on the third thin board, filling between them with buttercream. Measure and, using the wire cutters or heavy-duty scissors, cut dowels that are exactly the same height as the cake (C).

4. Insert the dowel rods into the bottom layer, evenly spaced about 4cm (1½in) in from the edge of the marked outline. Push the dowel rods straight down until each touches the cake board. The number of dowels to use depends on the size of the cake (D).

5. Apply a thin layer of buttercream on the top of the cake, just enough to cover the protruding dowels, then secure and stick the thin board to your cake drum using the glue. Do not just use buttercream or royal icing to stick the thin board to the drum as it could still slide about (E).

6. Repeat the process described in steps 3 and 4 to stack the other two cake sponges onto the glued-together thin boards, then position on top of the bottom two cakes (F).

7. Measure and cut a long dowel that is the height of the whole cake (G).

8. Insert the long dowel centrally right the way to the bottom of the cake (H).

COVERING CAKES

The first step, before you can add any wonderful decoration, is to know how to cover the cake, making sure that the buttercream sticks to it and provides a clean base. You need to crumb coat, and then create a smooth surface. Further techniques for creating textured surfaces can be found within the cake projects.

Crumb coating

Crumb coating means applying a thin layer of buttercream all over your cake to secure the loose crumbs. This is a very important step that you should not miss as this makes your outer layer of buttercream stick to the cake, giving the heavy piped and textured designs something to adhere to.

1. Use a round nozzle or just snip the end off a piping bag, then, using the same buttercream that will go on the rest of the cake, pipe around the cake with a good firm pressure so the buttercream sticks to the cake (I).

2. Use a palette knife to spread the buttercream all over the cake, applying even pressure and making sure to remove any excess buttercream with the edge of the palette knife (J).

3. You can use a cake scraper to even the thickness out or leave it as it is (K). Chill in the fridge or freezer for 15 to 30 minutes, or until the surface is firm to the touch.

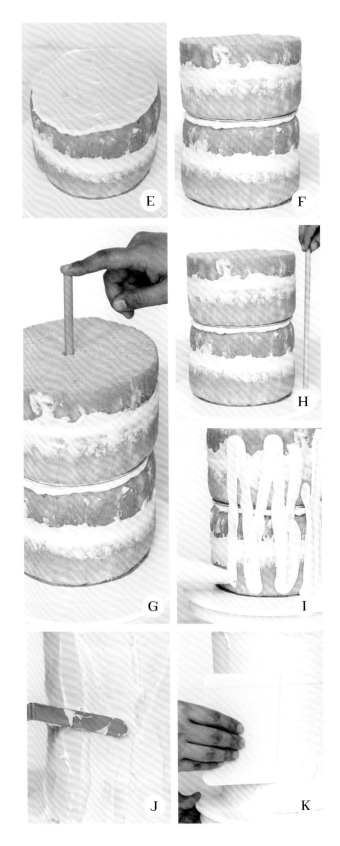

CAKE COVERING TIPS

- If our Queen of Hearts Cake Cloth is not available in your country, you may use a non-woven cloth, such as the interfacing used in sewing projects. This can be sourced online or from any reasonably large haberdashery.

- Do not place the cake in the fridge or freezer for hours or even overnight. This will make your cake very cold and as you bring it out of the fridge condensation or 'sweating' can occur due to the sudden rise in temperature.

- If you have finished a cake and you need to refrigerate it, make sure you place the cake in a box wrapped with cling film. Leave it in the box until you are ready to serve or display it.

- If you accidentally poke or scratch the surface of your cake several hours after it has been smoothed, *do not* smooth the surface with the Cake Cloth, as it will make the surface wrinkly because it has been crusted for a long time. Instead, dip the tip of a stainless palette knife into hot water and even out just that spot. You can expect that spot on the surface to have a slight colour difference due to the normal darkening process of drying buttercream.

Smoothing

Once the cake has been chilled and is firm, you are now ready to apply your final coating. The thickness of the buttercream is up to your preference. If the final coating is a single colour, you can use the same colour of buttercream for crumb coating. If the final coating is blended or multi-coloured, it is best to use plain (untinted) buttercream.

1. Apply the final coating of buttercream and spread it evenly with a palette knife (L).

2. Remove any excess and even out the thickness of the buttercream using a plain edge cake scraper. It is normal for the surface still to have some minor lines at this stage (M).

3. Let the cake dry at room temperature for about 5 to 10 minutes. To test if the surface is crusted, touch it gently. It is typical that you will see some oiliness, and as long as no buttercream sticks to your fingers, then it's ready (N).

4. When the cake is fully crusted, place a Cake Cloth on the surface and rub gently with your fingers to flatten any bumps and to smooth out any textures and creases. Repeat the same process all over the cake (O).

5. To make it even smoother, place the Cake Cloth back on the surface and use the scraper on top of it, running it up and down over the cloth (P).

6. Use a small knife, scraper or an angled palette knife to remove any excess buttercream on the edge of the cake. Let it crust again before smoothing it once more with the Cake Cloth (Q).

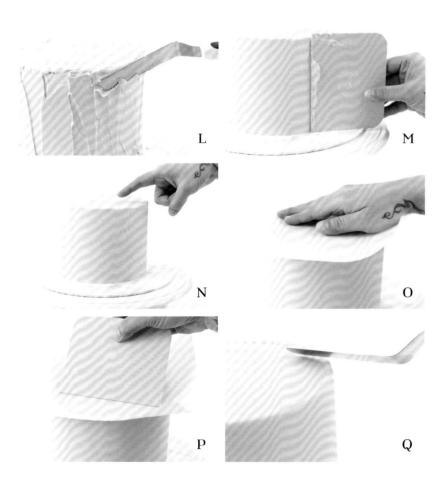

L

M

N

O

P

Q

Spring

VIOLET SPRINGTIME SPIRAL

A gentle cascade of violet, purple and pale pink flowers wrap this cake in a beautiful floral spiral. Gardeners' favourites, sweet peas, are piped directly onto the cake's surface in pretty pastel shades, as are the two-tone purple clematis, but you'll need to prepare the dramatically dark anemones in advance.

You will need

CAKE

- Top tier: 10cm (4in) round cake, 7.5cm (3in) high

- Middle tier: 15cm (6in) round cake, 15cm (6in) high

- Bottom tier: 20cm (8in) round cake, 15cm (6in) high

BUTTERCREAM

- 800g–1kg (1lb 12oz–2lb 4oz) white (Sugarflair Super White)

- 400g (14oz) light violet (Sugarflair Grape Violet + hint of Claret)

- 400g (14oz) dark violet buttercream (Sugarflair Grape Violet)

- 50g (1¾oz) black (Sugarflair Black)

- 400g (14oz) two-tone light and dark purple (Sugarflair Deep Violet)

- 50g (1¾oz) light caramel (Sugarflair Caramel)

- 300g (10½oz) pale violet (Sugarflair Grape Violet + hint of Blue)

- 300g (10½oz) light pink (Sugarflair Claret)

- 400g (14oz) very light green (Sugarflair Gooseberry)

- 400g (14oz) light green (Sugarflair Gooseberry)

- 500–600g (1lb 2oz–1lb 5oz) extra plain buttercream for blobs

EQUIPMENT

- Wilton petal nozzle 103

- Wilton petal nozzle 102

- Wilton leaf nozzle 352

- Piping bags

- Parchment paper/baking sheet

- Board or cookie tray

- Cake Cloth

- Cake scraper

- Toothpick (cocktail stick)

1. Stack and cover your cake with a smooth covering of white buttercream (see Cake Basics). Use dark and light violet buttercream to pipe the anemones onto parchment paper or a baking sheet in advance (see Piping Flowers). Don't pipe the anemone centres yet. Mark the shape of your floral spiral cascade by piping a thin line of white buttercream where you want the flowers to be arranged.

2. Starting at the bottom of each tier and working your way up, squeeze a small amount of buttercream to create an elongated blob where you want to place your anemones.

3. Using the Wilton petal nozzle 103, pipe your sweet peas (see Piping Flowers) directly on the cake using light pink and pale violet buttercream on each side of the blob. Leave spaces for the leaves.

4. Attach a few anemones to the blob, pressing from the centre to secure them. You may need a toothpick (cocktail stick) to help position them.

5. Pipe some leaves using the Wilton leaf nozzle 352 and light green and very light green buttercream (see Piping Flowers). Then pipe a flat blob for the clematis. You can pipe a guide circle to show the position of the clematis petals as well.

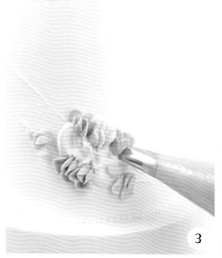

6. Using a Wilton leaf nozzle 352 with two-tone light and dark purple buttercream (see Buttercream Basics, Piping), pipe the clematis straight onto the cake (see Piping Flowers).

7. Repeat the same process as you follow your cascade guide line upwards. Pipe an elongated blob, more sweet peas and more leaves.

8. Always stick the anemone flowers on first so the clematis petals will overlap them.

9. Complete the spiralling cascade to the top of the cake.

6

7

8

9

TIP

When creating colours, you can mix and match by adding a hint of pink to the purple and vice versa, to achieve pleasingly complementing hues.

It is best to start at the bottom of the spiral and work your way up. In that way you can use the lower flowers to support the ones above.

10. Pipe the centres of the anemones using black buttercream in a piping bag with a small hole cut in the tip.

11. Pipe the centres of each clematis using light caramel buttercream in a piping bag with a small hole cut in the tip.

TIP

If you are not able to source the thin seamless type of piping bag (which are perfect for piping spikes), you can use writing nozzles 2 or 3.

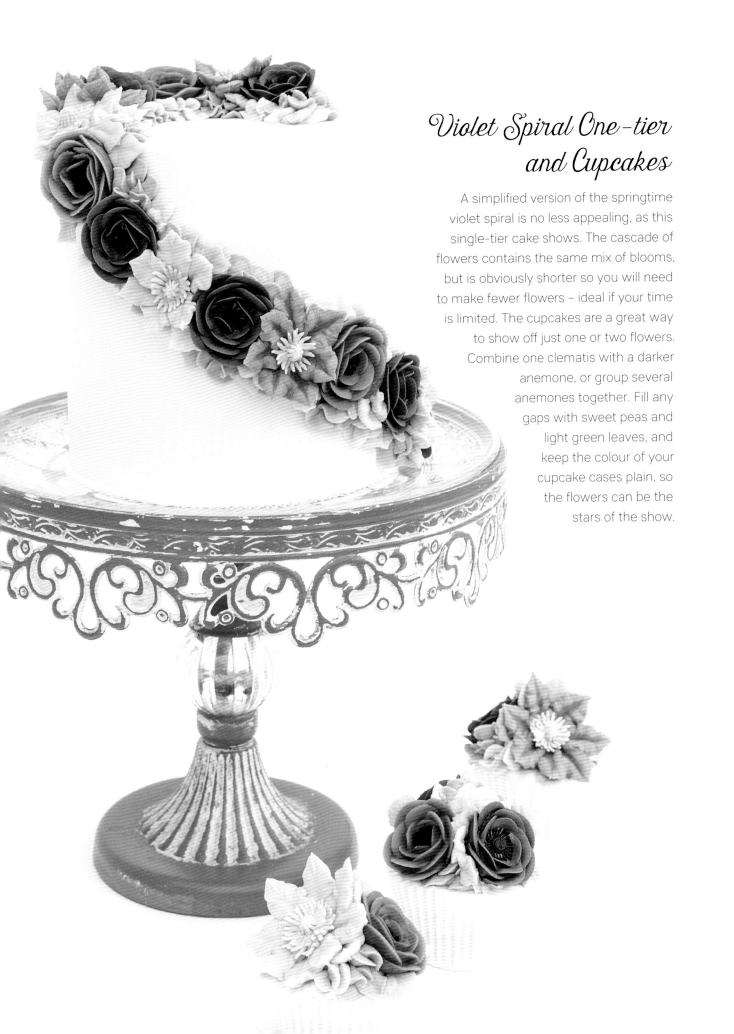

Violet Spiral One-tier and Cupcakes

A simplified version of the springtime violet spiral is no less appealing, as this single-tier cake shows. The cascade of flowers contains the same mix of blooms, but is obviously shorter so you will need to make fewer flowers – ideal if your time is limited. The cupcakes are a great way to show off just one or two flowers. Combine one clematis with a darker anemone, or group several anemones together. Fill any gaps with sweet peas and light green leaves, and keep the colour of your cupcake cases plain, so the flowers can be the stars of the show.

THE FULL FLORAL

The bursting bounty of springtime, when every shoot and bud comes to life, is perfectly captured in the exuberance of this design. The flowers crowd together, completely covering the cake surface, jostling with the fresh green leaves. It's the perfect show-stopper for a spring wedding!

You will need

CAKE

- Top tier: 10cm (4in) round cake, (7.5cm) 3in high
- Middle tier: 15cm (6in) round cake, (10cm) 4in high
- Bottom tier: 20cm (8in) round cake, (10cm) 4in high

BUTTERCREAM

- 500g (1lb 2oz) light pink (Sugarflair Claret)
- 1kg (2lb 4oz) light peach (Sugarflair Peach)
- 500g (1lb 2oz) light purple (Sugarflair Grape Violet)
- 600–800g (1lb 5oz–1lb 12oz) light green (Sugarflair Gooseberry)
- 300g (10½oz) pale green (Sugarflair Spruce Green)
- 100g (3½oz) dark yellow (Sugarflair Melon + hint of Autumn Leaf)
- 50g (1¾oz) light caramel (Sugarflair Caramel)
- 400–500g (14oz–1lb 2oz) light yellow (Sugarflair Melon + hint of Autumn Leaf)
- 500–600g (1lb 2oz–1lb 5oz) extra plain buttercream for blobs and crumb coating

EQUIPMENT

- Wilton petal nozzle 103
- Wilton petal nozzle 102
- Wilton chrysanthemum nozzle 81
- Wilton leaf nozzle 74
- Wilton leaf nozzle 352
- Piping bags
- Parchment paper/baking sheet
- Board or cookie tray
- Scissors

1. Pipe the camellias and chrysanthemums in advance: use light pink buttercream for the camellias, light peach for the peach ruffle flowers and light purple for the chrysanthemum flowers, and set aside (see Piping Flowers).

2. Stack and crumb coat the cake (see Cake Basics), then pipe thin blobs of plain buttercream all around the cake where you will position the flowers.

3. Pipe clusters of ruffles for leaves randomly all around the blobs using a Wilton leaf nozzle 74 with light green buttercream and a back and forth wiggle of the piping bag, but leave few spaces for the light yellow blossom flowers.

4. Pipe pulled petals for the yellow blossoms (see Piping Flowers) on some of the blobs using a Wilton petal nozzle 102 with light yellow buttercream.

5. Position all the ready-made flowers on the buttercream blobs. The blobs will need to be reasonably fresh so that flowers will adhere properly.

6. Pipe the centres of the flowers, using dark yellow for the chrysanthemums, light yellow for the camellias and light caramel for the yellow blossoms. Use a piping bag with a small hole cut at the tip for piping the centres.

7. Fill the rest of the gaps between flowers by piping pulled-petal-type leaves using a Wilton leaf nozzle 352 with pale green buttercream (see Piping Flowers).

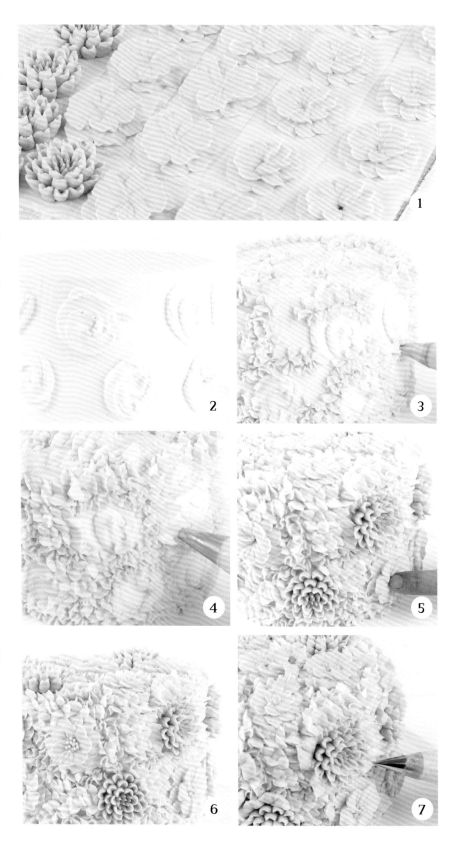

Full Floral One-tier and Cupcakes

The intensity of the flowers just seems to increase when they are on a smaller cake! Aim to fill every bit of the surface with flowers and ruffle leaves to get the full floral effect. Keep your cake stand or board simple to allow the cake to shine. The cupcakes should also appear crammed to bursting with blossoms.

SPRING WREATH

A pale and pretty wreath adorns this subtly marbled and textured cake. You'll need an angled palette knife to achieve the background effect, but it's simple to do and sets off the delicate floral arrangement beautifully. Pipe the main flowers in advance, then enhance them with foliage and buds that are piped directly onto the cake.

You will need

CAKE

- Top tier: 15 × 15cm (6 × 6in) square cake, 12.5cm (5in) high
- Bottom tier: 20 × 20cm (8 × 8in) square cake, 15cm (6in) high

BUTTERCREAM

- 800g–1kg (1lb 12oz–2lb 4oz) light caramel (Sugarflair Caramel)
- 100g (3½oz) slightly darker caramel (Sugarflair Caramel)
- 100g (3½oz) light green (Sugarflair Gooseberry)
- 600g (1lb 5oz) light peach (Sugarflair Peach)
- 600g (1lb 5oz) dark peach (Sugarflair Peach)
- 400g (14oz) light pink (Sugarflair Dusky Pink + hint of Claret)

- 400g (14oz) dark pink (Sugarflair Dusky Pink + hint of Claret)
- 50g (1¾oz) yellow (Sugarflair Autumn Leaf)
- 200g (7oz) white (Sugarflair Super White)
- 50g (1¾oz) brown (Sugarflair Dark Brown)
- 400g (14oz) very light green (Sugarflair Gooseberry + hint of Bitter Lemon)
- 400g (14oz) dark green (Sugarflair Spruce Green)
- 100g (3½oz) very pale green (Sugarflair Gooseberry)
- 100g (3½oz) very light pink (Sugarflair Dusky Pink)
- 500-600g (1lb 2oz–1lb 5oz) extra plain buttercream for blobs

EQUIPMENT

- Wilton petal nozzle 104
- Wilton petal nozzle 103
- Wilton petal nozzle 102
- Wilton petal nozzle 97
- Wilton leaf nozzle 352
- Wilton leaf nozzle 65s
- Angled palette knife
- Piping bags
- Parchment paper/baking sheet
- Board or cookie tray
- Toothpick (cocktail stick)

1. Pipe the ranunculus, open peonies and dogwood in advance: for the ranunculus use very light green buttercream (for the centres), light peach (for the inner petals) and dark peach (for the outer petals), use light and dark pink for the open peonies, and white buttercream for the dogwood (see Piping Flowers). You may find that piping the peony centres after they are attached to the cake is easier. Set them aside.

2. Crumb coat and stack your cakes (see Cake Basics), and apply a thin layer of light caramel buttercream onto the surface of the cake and even it out using an angled palette knife.

3. Using piping bags with a tiny hole cut at their tips, apply small blobs of slightly darker caramel and light green to the surface of the cake. Make sure you space them out evenly.

4. Using an angled palette knife, spread the small bobs with short up and down strokes to create a blended effect.

5. Pipe a guide line for the position of the wreath, using any tinted buttercream in a piping bag with a tiny hole at the tip.

TIP

If the buttercream surface is becoming dry and hard to spread, dip the tip of the palette knife into hot water and then continue. Make sure you shake off any excess water before doing so.

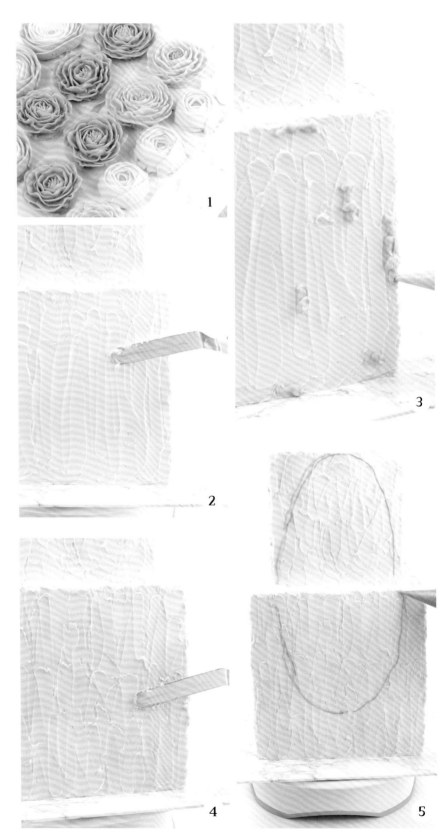

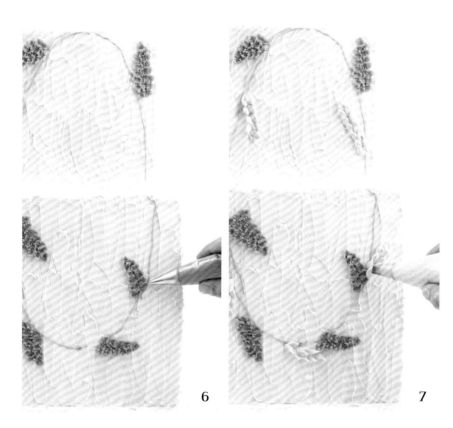

6. Pipe some ferns using the Wilton leaf nozzle 65s and dark green buttercream (see Piping Flowers).

7. Pipe more pulled petal style foliage (see Piping Flowers) using a Wilton petal nozzle 102 and very light green buttercream.

8. Next, position the pre-made ranunculus and open peonies that will go on the corners and edges of the ledge between the tiers, and parts where flowers can be more easily attached. Choose the heavier flowers to sit on horizontal surfaces. Then pipe some blobs of plain buttercream in other places where you want to attach your flowers.

9. Secure the rest of the ranunculus and open peonies to the blobs. Choose the smaller flowers for vertical surfaces as they are less likely to slide off the cake.

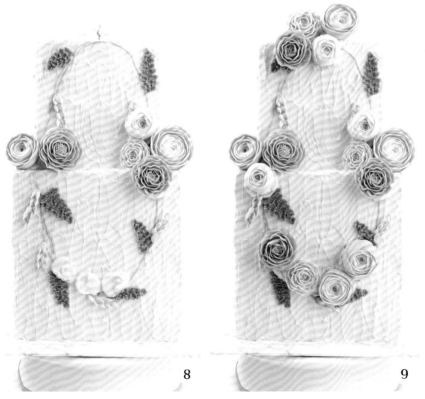

TIP

You can choose other types of foliage to provide variety (see Piping Flowers, Leaves). Check out photographs of real wreaths on the internet for inspiration. Just make sure you pipe the foliage first, before adding the flowers.

10. Pipe small blobs and position the pre-made dogwood flowers.

11. Using piping bags with a small hole cut at their tips, pipe the centres of the open peonies in yellow and the centres of the dogwood flowers using very light green buttercream. Then pipe some details on the dogwood petals using brown buttercream (see Piping Flowers).

12. Pipe very light green and dark green leaves around the wreath using a Wilton leaf nozzle 352.

13. Pipe tiny buds using very light green buttercream and very light pink buttercream in piping bags with a very small hole cut at their tips.

14. Cover up the buttercream blobs under the flowers at the top and the edges of the wreath with any remaining flowers and more leaves so that the blobs cannot be seen from any angle.

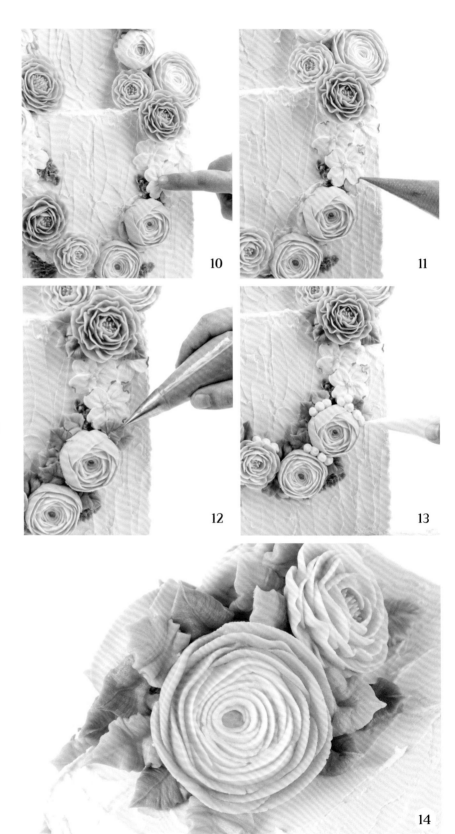

Spring Wreath One-tier and Cupcakes

We have chosen a square cake for the single-tier design, derived from the spring wreath cake. Group the flowers around two sides of the top of the cake, and allow dogwood blooms to creep round the remaining two sides. Fill the final corner with a rustic frame made by piping roughly woven lines with a round nozzle, or a medium hole cut at the tip of a piping bag, in brown buttercream. In reality you will need to pipe this frame first so that it appears 'behind' the flowers. The sweetly pretty cupcakes are perfect in pastel shades – just mix and match the flowers as you wish.

SPRING PASTEL CASCADE

Perfect in pastel shades, this tall cake will make a really show-stopping centrepiece for any springtime party table. Add a delicate cascade of flowers and foliage in colours to match each of the four tiers. Both the lisianthus and hydrangea flowers can be made in advance and frozen before you position them in the floral arrangements.

You will need

CAKE

- Top tier: 10cm (4in) round cake, 7.5cm (3in) high
- Upper middle tier: 15cm (6in) round cake, 10cm (4in) high
- Lower middle tier: 20cm (8in) round cake, 7.5cm (3in) high
- Bottom tier: 25cm (10in) round cake, 10cm (4in) high

BUTTERCREAM

- 300g (10½oz) light yellow (Sugarflair White base + hint of Sugarflair Egyptian Orange)
- 400g (14oz) light pink (Sugarflair White base + hint of Sugarflair Dusky Pink)
- 500g (1lb 2oz) light purple (Sugarflair White base + hint of Sugarflair Dusky Pink)
- 600g (1lb 5oz) light blue (Sugarflair White base + hint of Sugarflair Navy Blue + hint of Sugarflair Baby Blue)
- 100g (3½oz) dark yellow (Sugarflair Melon Yellow + Sugarflair Autumn Leaf)
- 200g (7oz) of each of the tier colours in slightly darker and lighter shades for the hydrangea and lisianthus flowers
- 100g (3½oz) green (Sugarflair Gooseberry)
- 200g (7oz) darker green (Sugarflair White base + hint of Sugarflair Spruce Green)
- 200g (7oz) light yellow-green (Sugarflair White base + hint of Sugarflair Gooseberry)
- 400g (14oz) light green (Sugarflair White base + hint of Sugarflair Gooseberry)
- 100g (3½oz) white (Sugarflair White)

EQUIPMENT

- Wilton petal nozzle 104
- Wilton petal nozzle 103
- Wilton leaf nozzle 352
- Wilton star nozzle 14
- Angled palette knife
- Cake scraper
- Wilton cake comb (design of your choice)
- Cake Cloth
- Piping bags
- Parchment paper
- Board or cookie tray
- Scissors
- Toothpicks (cocktail sticks)

1. Pipe the lisianthus flowers in advance in shades to match the layers of the cake (see Piping Flowers). Crumb coat the cakes (see Cake Basics), then apply a generous amount of buttercream with the palette knife to cover all tiers, using light yellow for the top tier and light pink, purple and blue for the other tiers (see photograph of finished cake). Even out the thickness of buttercream as you prepare each tier, and remove any excess with a plain edge cake scraper. Hold the cake comb at about 60 degrees to the surface and run the edge around your cake to form ridges. Use a turntable while working to keep movement and pattern smooth. Repeat the process until the design is even and the pattern complete.

2. Leave the cake top plain and even, let it crust for 3–5 minutes and smooth with a cake cloth.

3. Dowel and stack the cakes (see Cake Basics), then pipe a border of dots at the bottom of each tier, using matching buttercream in a piping bag with a small hole at the tip.

4. Using green in a piping bag with a small hole at the tip, pipe guide marks for the position of the long leaves and veronica flowers. Some of these guides will become the centre stems for the long leaves.

5. To pipe the long leaves, use darker green buttercream and position the wide end of the petal nozzle 103 on the guide line (the centre stem of the leaf). Continuously squeeze the piping bag as you slowly pull the nozzle away from the cake. Make sure you release the pressure when you reach the desired length for the leaf. Repeat the process to create alternating leaves.

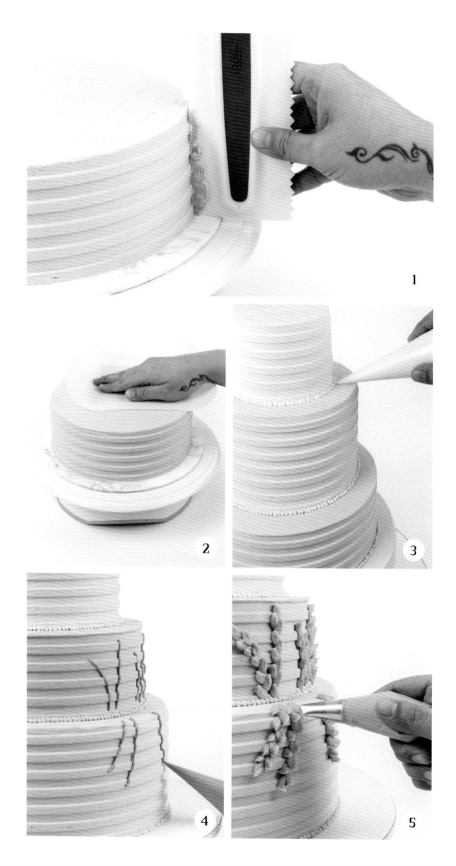

SPRING PASTEL CASCADE

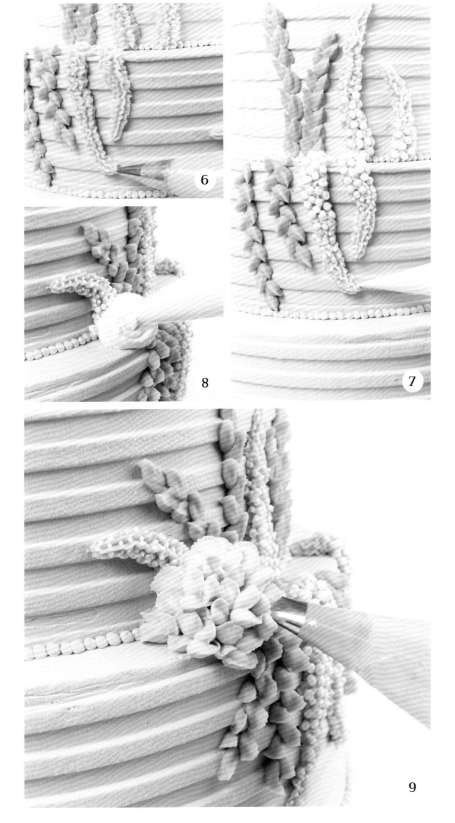

6. To pipe the veronica flowers, use light yellow-green buttercream in a piping bag with the star nozzle 14. Starting at the base of the flower, give the piping bag a good firm squeeze while slowly pulling the nozzle in the desired direction, letting the buttercream build up slightly. Reduce the pressure on the piping bag as you move towards the tip of the flower. You are aiming for an elongated and slightly curvy teardrop shape with a pointy tip.

7. Using white buttercream in a piping bag with a small hole at the tip, pipe medium-sized dots, starting at the base of the veronica flowers and decreasing in size towards the tip.

8. Position your hydrangeas if you have pre-piped and frozen them, lifting them from the parchment paper with scissors and fixing them to the cake with a fresh blob of buttercream. Alternatively, if you are piping them directly onto the cake, make sure to pipe a big round blob of buttercream as a base for the flower.

9. Use the simple petal stroke technique (see Piping Flowers) with the petal nozzle 103 to pipe your hydrangeas, matching the flower colour to the colour of each tier. Use each buttercream colour with light green to create a two-tone effect for the hydrangea petals (see Buttercream Basics, Piping).

10. Pipe small dots in the centre of each of the flowers in the hydrangea blooms using light green buttercream in a piping bag with a small hole at the tip.

11. Pipe small blobs of buttercream before positioning the rest of the flowers.

12. Position and secure the lisianthus flowers to match the colours of the tiers. You might find that using two toothpicks (cocktail sticks) can help to manoeuvre the flowers into position without damaging them.

13. Pipe some small leaves the fill in some of the gaps between the flowers using the leaf nozzle 352 and light green buttercream.

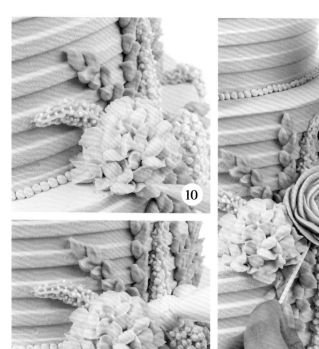

TIP

You can pre-pipe all the lisianthus flowers ahead of time and place them on a board or cookie tray lined with parchment paper and place them in the freezer 10–15 minutes before arranging them on the cake. To pipe them, use the upright petal stroke technique (see Piping Flowers) with dark yellow spikes at the centre. You can also pipe and freeze the hydrangeas, or pipe them directly on the cake.

Spring Pastel One-tier and Cupcakes

Instead of using a colour present in any of the flowers, we have chosen light green to cover the one-tier cake to complement the flowers, and to provide a fresh-looking backdrop to their springtime abundance. Although we used the same cake comb design as the main cake, there are many different variations on the market that you could choose. You don't even need a cake comb, but could add some interesting grass-like texture using a simple fork.

Arrange lisianthus and hydrangea blossoms in clusters on the top of the cupcakes, and add plenty of light green foliage to fill the gaps – they should look as if they are bursting with beautiful flowers!

Summer

OUR NAKED CAKE

Cakes that wear their insides on the outside are very fashionable, so we couldn't resist baring one of our own! It's a beautiful way to use ombre colours on the stacked cakes, so the shade of the sponge changes from top to bottom. A modest ruffle tidies up the filling between the layers, and tulips and scabious add all the frothy decadence of summer, around the ledge between the tiers and on the very top of the cake.

You will need

CAKE

- Top tier: three 15cm (6in) round cakes, 7.5cm (3in) high, ombre green (see photograph for guidance on colouring)

- Bottom tier: four 20cm (8in) round cakes, 10cm (4in) high, ombre green (see photograph for guidance on colouring)

BUTTERCREAM

- 250–300g (9–10½oz) light pink (Sugarflair Pink + hint of Orange)

- 250–300g (9–10½oz) dark pink (Sugarflair Pink + hint of Orange)

- 50g (1¾oz) dark yellow (Sugarflair Melon + hint of Autumn Leaf)

- 150g (5½oz) light purple (Sugarflair Grape Violet)

- 150g (5½oz) dark purple (Sugarflair Grape Violet)

- 50g (1¾oz) pale green (Sugarflair Caramel + hint of Gooseberry)

- 100g (3½oz) white (Sugarflair Super White)

- 500–600g (1lb 2oz–1lb 5oz) dark green (Sugarflair Spruce Green)

- 500–600g (1lb 2oz–1lb 5oz) light green (Sugarflair Gooseberry)

- 1.5–1.8kg (3lb 5oz–4lb) extra plain buttercream for blobs, filling and ruffles

EQUIPMENT

- Wilton petal nozzle 104

- Wilton petal nozzle 103

- Wilton petal nozzle 102

- Wilton leaf nozzle 352

- Wilton chrysanthemum nozzle 81

- Piping bags

- Parchment paper/baking sheet

- Board or cookie tray

- Scissors

- Narrow tip palette knife

1. First make your main flowers in advance (see Piping Flowers), varying their sizes a little: use light and dark pink buttercream for the tulips and give them dark yellow centres, and use light and dark purple for the scabious flowers, giving them pale green centres. Stack the cakes (see Cake Basics) making sure the darkest shade of the cake is at the bottom and the layers get lighter as you go towards the top.

2. Apply a little more plain buttercream around the edges, in between the tiers, to ensure that all the gaps are filled properly.

3. Using a small narrow tip palette knife, even out and flatten the buttercream in between the tiers. Remember that you are not aiming to cover too much of the cake sides.

4. Using more plain buttercream and a Wilton petal nozzle 102, with the wide end of the nozzle touching the filling and narrow end pointing upwards, steadily squeeze the piping bag with slight up and down motion to create upright ruffles. Repeat the same process for all the fillings between layers.

TIP

If you need to keep the cake overnight, before you add the flowers put it in an airtight box and wrap it in cling film so that the cake sponges don't dry out.

As a variation, you can make the cake sponges plain in colour, but create the ombre effect with the buttercream that you use for the filling and ruffles.

5. Using the same nozzle, repeat the same process with the nozzle positioned upside down. Pipe downward ruffles making sure that the downward ones touch the upright ones.

6. Use more plain buttercream and a piping bag with a tiny hole at the tip to pipe beads in between the ruffles.

7. Pipe some blobs of plain buttercream in between the tiers where you want to secure the tulips.

8. Position the tulips in between the tiers, randomly adding small and big ones. Pipe light and dark green leaves (see Piping Flowers) in between the tulips using Wilton leaf nozzle 352.

TIP

Make sure that you pipe the tulips small enough so that they will easily fit in the small space in between the tiers. This will also prevent them becoming so heavy that they pull at the cake, making cracks in the naked sponges.

9. Pipe a fairly flat mound of buttercream on the top of the cake and position the scabious on it, making sure that the mound of buttercream is not too high. Position tulips in between the scabious.

10. Pipe more leaves to cover the gaps in between the flowers and previously piped leaves.

11. Using a piping bag filled with white buttercream and with a tiny hole at the end and the pressure piping technique (see Piping Flowers), pipe baby's breath flowers as tiny dots, ideally in between leaves.

Naked One-tier and Cupcakes

No ombre effect on the one-tier version of the naked cake, but the crumb coating of the top of the cake thins at the sides so that you can still see an enticing glimpse of sponge – it's known as a semi-naked cake. The flowers still crowd on top and frame the base of the cake, but the delicate piped patterns and the one word 'Love' are what steal the show here. We've taken the cupcakes out of their cases and turned them upside down to create a plinth to display some tulips and scabious flowers.

DAHLIAS ON DISPLAY

The muted brown of the rough burlap effect makes the colours of these pompom dahlias and green carnations really zing. It's the perfect background for any brightly coloured flowers, and is quite easy to make, using versatile cake lace. So get your dazzling dahlias on display for a cheerful cake that will make anyone smile!

You will need

CAKE

- Top tier: 15cm (6in) round cake, 15cm (6in) high
- Bottom tier: 20cm (10in) round cake, 10cm (4in) high

BUTTERCREAM

- 700-800g (1lb 9oz–1lb 12oz) white (Sugarflair Super White)
- 500–600g (1lb 2oz–1lb 5oz) bright green (Sugarflair Bitter Lemon + hint of Gooseberry)
- 300–400g (10½–14oz) yellow (Sugarflair Melon + hint of Autumn Leaf)
- 300–400g (10½–14oz) yellow-orange (Sugarflair Orange + Autumn Leaf)
- 300–400g (10½–14oz) orange (Sugarflair Orange + hint of Red)
- 300–400g (10½–14oz) red (Sugarflair Red Extra)
- 150–300g (5½–10½oz) light pink (Sugarflair Claret)
- 150–300g (5½–10½oz) dark pink (Sugarflair Claret)
- 500–600g (1lb 2oz–1lb 5oz) dark green (Sugarflair Spruce Green)
- 800g–1kg (1lb 12oz–2lb 4oz) extra plain buttercream for blobs

EQUIPMENT

- Wilton petal nozzle 101
- Wilton petal nozzle 102
- Wilton leaf nozzle 352
- Piping bags
- Parchment paper/baking sheet
- Board or cookie tray
- Scissors
- Burlap pattern silicone mat
- Cake lace, tinted brown
- Florist wire, 24 or 26 gauge
- Safety Seal food-safe barrier, or kitchen foil
- Cake Cloth
- Cake scraper
- Angled palette knife
- Toothpick (cocktail stick)
- Scissors
- Ruler
- Paint brush
- Piping gel

1. Pipe the dahlias and carnations in advance: the dahlias in yellow, yellow-orange, orange, red, light pink and dark pink buttercream, and the carnations in bright green (see Piping Flowers).

2. Stack and cover your cakes, giving them a smooth coat of white buttercream (see Cake Basics). Prepare the burlap-effect cake lace ahead of time too. Use the burlap pattern silicone mat and cake lace tinted brown to create a sheet of 'burlap'. Cut the burlap to the following sizes: two pieces 9 × 23cm (3½ × 9in), two pieces 7.5 × 33cm (3 × 13in), two squares 9 × 9cm (3½ × 3½in), two 9 × 2cm (3½ × ¾in) strips, and some extra thin strips.

3. Create a bow from a 9 × 9cm (3½ × 3½in) square by folding and pinching the centre.

4. Use a length of florist wire to tie the bow in the middle. Twist the two ends of the wire together and leave about 2.5cm (1in) excess before you trim it.

TIP

When making the cake lace we used Sugarflair Dark Brown colouring to give it the right shade. Just follow the simple colouring instructions on the cake lace packaging. Make it a shade or two lighter than your final desired colour as it tends to become darker after you bake it.

1

2

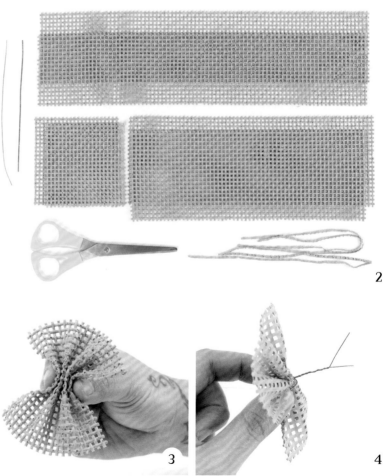

3

4

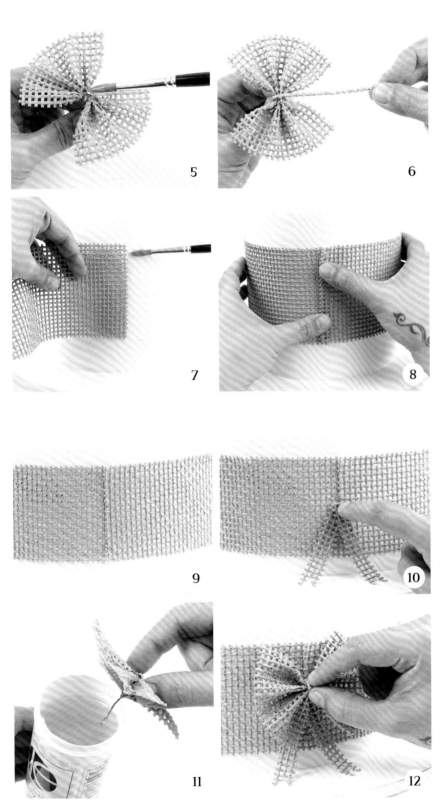

5. Use a paint brush to apply piping gel around the middle of the bow.

6. Wrap a thin strip of burlap around the centre of the bow to cover the wire.

7. Mark with piping gel where you will position the burlap on the top tier, making sure the gel is within the actual size of the 'burlap' band, so that it does not show. Then apply a thin, even layer of piping gel all over where you will attach the burlap.

8. Position the burlap, pressing gently until it slightly overlaps at the front of the cake.

9. Repeat the same process on the bottom tier.

10. Take the two 9 × 2cm (3½ × ¾in) strips of burlap and cut a 'v' shape at one end of each for the tail of the ribbon. Stick them on the side of the bottom tier with a thin layer of piping gel, as shown.

11. Dip the end of the florist wire in the Safety Seal until it develops a thick barrier. Alternatively, you can wrap a piece of kitchen foil around the wire.

12. Attach the ribbon. Make sure to poke its wire through the tops of the ribbon tails to add support.

13. Take a thin strip of cake lace and 'stitch' it through the seams of the 'burlap' band on the top tier. Space your 'stitches' about 2–3 squares apart and use a toothpick (cocktail stick) to help you insert the strips into the small holes.

14. Cut short pieces of another thin strip and pipe a dot of piping gel onto the middle of each piece, then insert them inside the loops of the 'stitches'.

15. Pipe blobs of plain buttercream to position the dahlias and carnations.

16. Position the colourful dahlias and green carnations randomly, some on top of each other. Secure the flowers to the blobs by gently pressing them in the centre.

17. Pipe the centres of the dahlias using piping bags with a small hole at the tip and the leftover orange and yellow buttercream.

18. Using the Wilton leaf nozzle 352, pipe dark green leaves in the gaps in between the flowers.

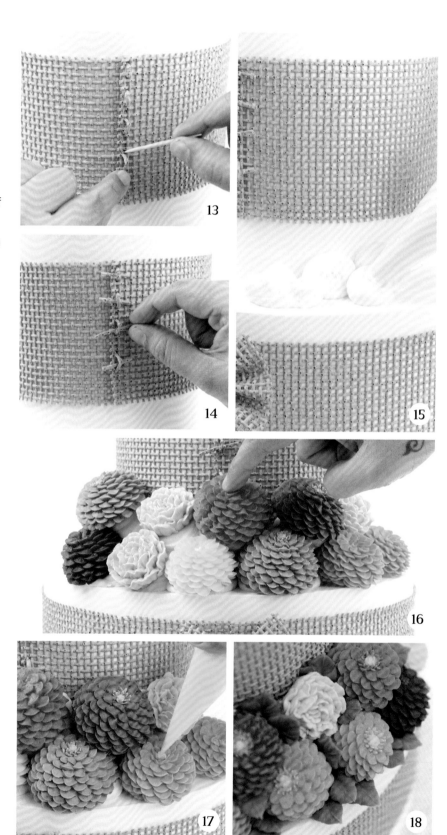

Dahlias on Display
One-tier and Cupcakes

A tall single-tier cake with a wide 'burlap band' is a great way to show off a vibrant arrangement of perfectly piped dahlias. There's no need to add more flowers to the base. We have placed our one-tier dahlia cake on a rough sawn log to complement the natural-looking burlap. The cupcakes have been made in dark-coloured cases, which really makes the bright palette of the flowers pop.

BIRDCAGE BOUQUET

With tier upon tier of glorious summer flowers, this cake reaches a crescendo with an elegant domed top supporting lavender, roses, billy ball flowers, gerbera daisies, sunflowers and hydrangea blossoms. We have used the lavender flower spikes to suggest the bars of a vintage birdcage, evenly spaced and delicate.

You will need

CAKE

- Top tier: 15cm (6in) half-ball dome cake
- Upper middle tier: 15cm (6in) round cake, 7.5cm (3in) high
- Lower middle tier: 20cm (8in) round cake, 7.5cm (3in) high
- Bottom tier: 25cm (10in) round cake, 10cm (4in) high

BUTTERCREAM

- 800g–1kg (1lb 12oz–2lb 4oz) very light caramel (Sugarflair Super White + hint of Caramel)
- 300g (10½oz) light blue (Sugarflair Baby Blue)
- 300g (10½oz) white (Sugarflair Super White)
- 300g (10½oz) light orange (Sugarflair Tangerine)

- 300g (10½oz) dark orange (Sugarflair Tangerine + hint of Red)
- 600g (1lb 5oz) yellow (Sugarflair Melon + hint of Autumn Leaf)
- 50g (1¾oz) black (Sugarflair Black)
- 100g (3½oz) dark yellow (Sugarflair Autumn Leaf)
- 400g (14oz) light pink (Sugarflair Dusky Pink + Orange)
- 400g (14oz) dark pink (Sugarflair Dusky Pink + hint of Orange)
- 100g (3½oz) light purple (Sugarflair Grape Violet + hint of Claret)
- 100g (3½oz) dark purple (Sugarflair Grape Violet)
- 400g (14oz) very light green (Sugarflair Gooseberry + hint of White)

- 500–600g (1lb 2oz–1lb 5oz) extra plain buttercream for blobs

EQUIPMENT

- Wilton petal nozzle 104
- Wilton petal nozzle 103
- Wilton chrysanthemum nozzle 81
- Wilton leaf nozzle 65s
- Wilton leaf nozzle 352
- Piping bags
- Parchment paper/baking sheet
- Board or cookie tray
- Scissors
- Piece of paper/card
- Cake Cloth
- Cake scraper
- Angled palette knife

1. We used a 15cm (6in) ball pan for the domed top of the cake.

2. Stack and cover the cakes, giving them a smooth covering of very light caramel buttercream (see Cake Basics). For the domed part of the cake, use a bendy scraper or square of flexible plastic and curve the scraper as you move your hand.

3. When smoothing the dome with the Cake Cloth, follow the curves of the cake and work on small areas at a time. Be careful not to make folds or creases in the cloth.

4. Pipe your main flowers and some leaves in advance: use very light green for the leaves, two-tone white and light blue (see Buttercream Basics, Piping) for the hydrangeas, yellow for the billy ball flowers, and light and dark pink for the David Austin roses (see Piping Flowers). Pipe the lavender straight onto the surface of the cake using dark and light purple buttercream in a piping bag with a small hole at the tip (see Piping Flowers). Evenly space the lavender flower spikes out as if they are the bars of the birdcage, with a flower spike from the top reaching towards a matching spike below.

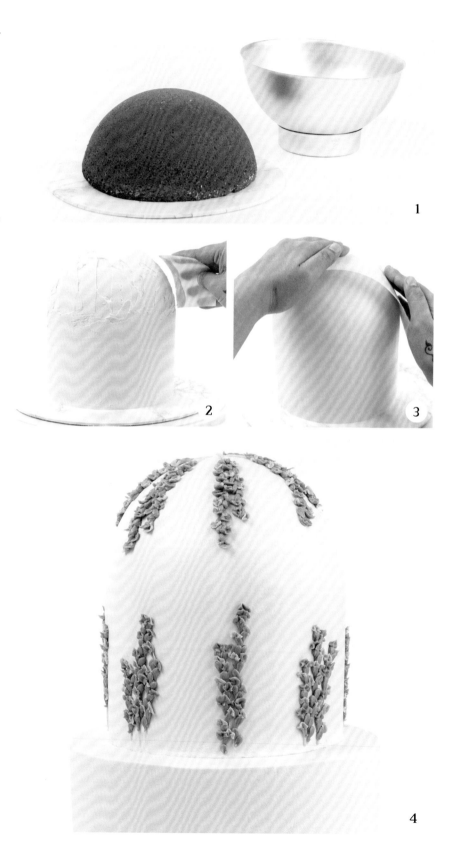

5. Pipe some very light green foliage next to the lavender, using a piping bag with a 'v' shape cut out at the tip. You can pipe guide marks to follow before you start if you find that easier.

6. Pipe thin blobs of plain buttercream and position the pre-made leaves onto them.

7. Pipe flat-topped blobs of buttercream of a suitable size for the rest of the pre-piped flowers, making sure they are evenly spaced around the cake.

8. Position and secure the pre-piped hydrangeas, David Austin roses and billy ball flowers. Pipe the hydrangea centres in very light green using a piping bag with a small hole at the tip. Place some flowers on the top of the birdcage as well.

9. Pipe the gerbera daisies directly onto the cake (see Piping Flowers), some in light and some in dark orange. Pipe the centres in yellow and black buttercream using a piping bag with a small hole at the tip. If a daisy's position makes it partially obscured by another flower, you can just pipe half or three-quarters of the daisy.

TIP

When you want to place pre-piped leaves on an edge, it is best to let the leaves dry out and harden first so that after positioning them they stay rigid. Or just make sure that the leaves are well supported by a surface, and not hanging off the cake too much, so that they don't begin to curve out or downwards.

10. Pipe the sunflowers in dark yellow and their centres in brown buttercream (see Piping Flowers).

11. Finish off the cake by piping clusters of baby's breath (see Piping Flowers, Pressure Piping) using a piping bag with a small hole at the tip and white buttercream.

10

TIP

For the baby's breath flowers, you can also mix dots and small stars using Wilton star nozzle 13 or 14 as a variation.

11

Birdcage Bouquet
One-tier and Cupcakes

The domed part of this design is definitely our favourite element, so naturally we chose to develop it for our one-tier version of the cake. Create this cake in the same way as the top tier of the full size example, dress it with lavender and pile the top and base with sunflowers, hydrangeas, gerbera daisies and roses. Bright green cupcake cases show off small clusters of the same selection of flowers to perfection.

SUMMER SUCCULENTS

We've crammed as many cacti and succulents onto this cake as we possibly could! When you make your own version you can mix and match the colours and don't just stick to the ones we did – that's why we haven't specified which colour to use in every case, but mostly just given you a list of suggested colours. Look at real succulents to get your inspiration. This is the perfect cake for anyone creative who loves intriguing design and something a bit out of the ordinary.

You will need

CAKE

- Each tier (two cakes in total): 20cm (8in) square cake, 10cm (4in) high

BUTTERCREAM

- 700g (1lb 9oz) light caramel (Sugarflair White base + Caramel)

- 100g (3½oz) brown (Sugarflair Dark Brown)

- 300–400g (10½–14oz) each of several shades of green and purple for cacti and succulents (Sugarflair White base + Gooseberry, and Sugarflair White base + Spruce Green, and Sugarflair White base + Khaki, and Sugarflair Spruce Green + hint of White, and Sugarflair Spruce Green + Eucalyptus, and Sugarflair White base + hint

of Grape Violet, and Sugarflair Burgundy, and Sugarflair Autumn Leaf + Burgundy, and Sugarflair Gooseberry)

- 100g (3½oz) dark pink (Sugarflair White base + hint of Claret)

- 500–600g (1lb 2oz–1lb 5oz) extra plain buttercream for blobs

EQUIPMENT

- Wilton petal nozzle 101
- Wilton petal nozzle 102
- Wilton petal nozzle 103
- Wilton petal nozzle 150
- Wilton leaf nozzle 352
- Wilton star nozzle 14
- Wilton big star nozzle 2D

- Wilton star nozzle 23
- Wilton round nozzle 8
- Wilton round nozzle 5 (optional)
- Piece of paper, at least 20 × 20cm (8 × 8in) square
- Serrated knife
- Piping bags
- Parchment paper/baking sheet
- Board or cookie tray
- Scissors
- Piece of flexible plastic
- Cake Cloth
- Cake scraper
- Angled palette knife

1. Pipe a selection of cacti and succulents in a variety of greens and purples, such as those listed in the you will need, with various nozzles (see Piping Flowers), and set them aside.

2. Make the top of your cakes perfectly flat by cutting off any excess bulge with a serrated knife. Next, make a 20 × 20cm (8 × 8in) square template out of paper and fold twice to create four equal quadrants. Cut one of the quadrants out, then place the template over one of the cakes and cut out a quadrant of cake.

3. Fill and stack your cakes (see Cake Basics) and place the cut-out piece of cake on the top corner.

4. Crumb coat your cake and cover with light caramel buttercream (see Cake Basics). Apply small blobs of brown buttercream, mostly on the edges and corners, then lightly spread with an angled palette knife using vertical (up and down) strokes.

5. Even out and blend the colours using a small piece of flexible plastic as a scraper. Use up and down strokes but do not overdo it. You want the marbled effect to show.

6. Lightly smooth your cake with a small piece of Cake Cloth.

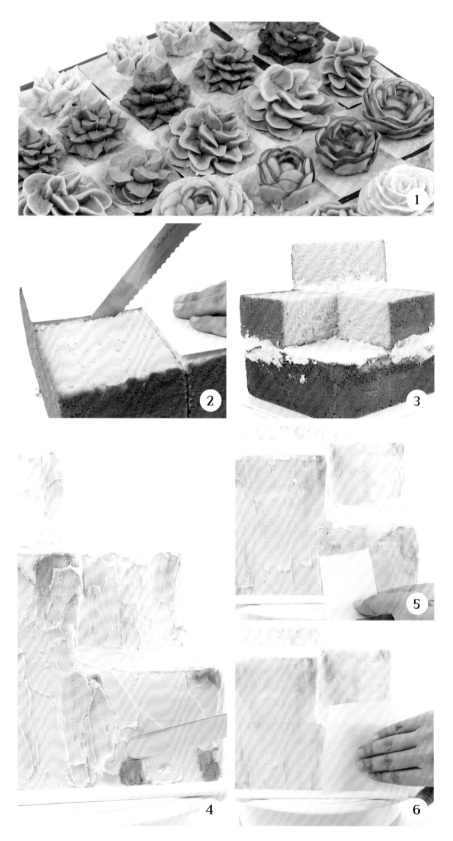

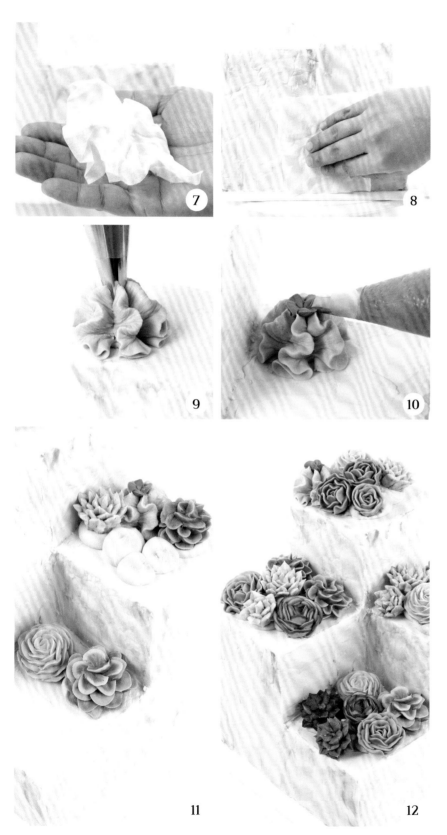

7. Crumple a piece of Cake Cloth.

8. Gently press the crumpled Cake Cloth on some parts of the cake to get a weathered look. Do not overdo it. It is nice to see some smooth parts here and there around the cake.

9. Pipe a cactus using Wilton big star nozzle 2D. Hold the piping bag straight with the opening of the nozzle flat to the cake surface and steadily squeeze the bag as you slowly pull away. Stop when you have created the size of the cactus you desire.

10. Pipe a five-petal flower on top of the cactus using dark pink buttercream with a Wilton petal nozzle 102.

11. Pipe small blobs of caramel buttercream and secure your pre-piped succulents and cacti, in no particular order.

12. Arrange the rest of your plants until you have filled all the spaces.

13. Pipe some long pointy cacti to fill some of the gaps. Use a Wilton star nozzle 23 and use the same technique that you would for piping a pulled-petal-type leaf (see Piping Flowers).

14. Pipe some different cacti using a Wilton star nozzle 14 and two-tone buttercream (see Buttercream Basics, Piping) with the same leaf piping technique, but slightly twisting your hand as you slowly pull the piping bag away.

15. Pipe plain but pointy cacti with light green buttercream and a Wilton round nozzle 8 or 10 to fill some other gaps, and other cacti with a Wilton round nozzle 8 using the pulled piping technique.

16. Fill more gaps by piping spikes using dark yellow buttercream in a plain piping bag with a medium hole at the tip (or you can use a Wilton round nozzle 5).

17. Pipe some buds with light purple centres using a plain piping bag with a small hole at the tip.

18. Finally, pipe some small ruffles or wavy upright petals (see Piping Flowers) using red buttercream with a Wilton petal nozzle 101.

Boxed Succulents One-tier and Cupcakes

This neat box realistically evokes the way that hardy little succulents are often grown, and shows off their curious structures and range of colours perfectly. The box itself is covered and coloured just like the main cake, but with a smooth surface, except for the 'planks' and 'nails' on the sides. Divide the top of the box into nine equal spaces, then use the smooth side of a Wilton basketweave nozzle 47 to pipe three or four 'stripes' on top of each other to create raised partitions before adding your succulents. The cupcakes that match are covered with the whole spectrum of greens and purples – have fun making up your own mini plants, inspired by nature.

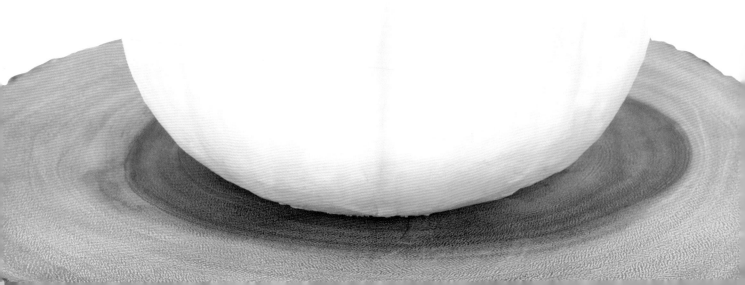

Autumn

OPULENT AUTUMN CASCADE

There's a decadent richness to this design, which you may choose to reflect in the cake beneath the buttercream. Why not use a classic red velvet cake recipe to match the gorgeous crimson roses, amaranthus and dahlias? The swathe of red, white and gold flowers rests on an off-white ruffled background – impressive, but simple to pipe when you know how.

You will need

CAKE

- Top tier: 10cm (4in) round cake, 7.5cm (3in) high
- Middle tier: 15cm (6in) round cake, 10cm (4in) high
- Bottom tier: 20cm (8in) round cake, 10cm (4in) high

BUTTERCREAM

- 500–600g (1lb 2oz–1lb 5oz) very light caramel (Sugarflair Caramel)
- 400g (14oz) dark red (Sugarflair Red Extra + hint of Black)
- 500g (1lb 2oz) crimson red (Sugarflair Red Extra + Claret)
- 400g (14oz) red-orange (Sugarflair Red Extra + Orange)
- 300g (10½oz) dark caramel (Sugarflair Caramel)
- 100g (3½oz) light caramel (Sugarflair Caramel)
- 300g (10½oz) dark green (Sugarflair Spruce Green)
- 100g (3½oz) light brown (Sugarflair Dark Brown)
- 200g (7oz) light olive green (Sugarflair Gooseberry + hint of Brown)
- 200g (7oz) yellow (Sugarflair Melon + hint of Autumn Leaf)
- 100–200g (3½–7oz) dark purple (Sugarflair Grape Violet + Black)
- 500–600g (1lb 2oz–1lb 5oz) extra plain buttercream for blobs

EQUIPMENT

- Wilton petal nozzle 124
- Wilton petal nozzle 104
- Wilton petal nozzle 101
- Wilton petal nozzle 150
- Wilton chrysanthemum nozzle 81
- Wilton star nozzle 14
- Wilton leaf nozzle 352
- Wilton writing nozzle 2 (optional)
- Piping bags
- Parchment paper/baking sheet
- Board or cookie tray
- Scissors
- DinkyDoodle Shell & Shine
- Cake Cloth
- Cake scraper
- Angled palette knife

1. Make the roses, dahlias, poppy heads and some leaves in advance: use crimson red for the roses, red-orange for the dahlias, light and dark caramel for the poppy heads, and dark green for the round leaves (see Piping Flowers). These leaves are piped with a Wilton petal nozzle 124, then spray glazed with Shell & Shine.

2. Next, pipe straight but short ruffles starting at the top edge of each of the cake. Using very light caramel buttercream and a Wilton petal nozzle 150, place the nozzle onto the side of the cake so that the opening is slightly tilted towards the surface. Steadily squeeze the piping bag as you drag it away. Each ruffle needs to slightly overlap the previous one.

3. Always pipe the succeeding layers of ruffles slightly below the previous ruffle, making sure that the lower part of the nozzle is touching the surface of the cake. Avoid too much squeezing so ruffles do not become wavy.

4. Pipe a guide for the red amaranthus. Using Wilton star nozzle 14 and dark red buttercream, continuously squeeze the piping bag, starting from the top edge of the cake as you slowly drag downwards, at the same time slightly turning the nozzle to give a more textured look.

5. Pipe the twigs using a piping bag with a small hole at the tip and light brown buttercream.

6. Pipe a thin blob of plain buttercream and position the pre-piped round leaves. Press lightly to make sure they adhere to the surface properly.

7. Arrange the flowers starting from the bottom tier. Pipe some buttercream blobs, then position the roses and poppy heads.

8. Carry on arranging the floral elements by adding the dahlias and piping buttercream blobs ready for the sunflowers.

9. The flowers should decrease in density towards the top of the cake to create a cascade look.

10. Pipe the sunflowers directly on the cake using a Wilton leaf nozzle 352 and yellow buttercream for the petals and giving them light brown centres (see Piping Flowers).

11. Pipe leaves in between the flowers using a Wilton leaf nozzle 352 and light olive green buttercream (see Piping Flowers).

TIP

Due to the quantity of floral details on this cake, it is best to keep the background ruffles straight, rather than wavy, as they could clash with the flowers. If you would prefer a wavy ruffle design, reduce the floral details and use Wilton petal nozzle 104 instead of 150.

12. To fill any gaps, pipe berries in dark purple with a piping bag with a hole at the tip, or you can use a Wilton writing nozzle 2.

13. Pipe the centres of the dahlias with yellow buttercream in a piping bag with a hole at the tip.

12

TIP

Be careful when mixing red tinted buttercream as it has a tendency to become really dark as it dries and firms up. Make it a shade lighter and give it an hour or two to settle before piping.

13

Opulent Autumn Cascade
One-tier and Cupcakes

The design of the large three-tier cake translates beautifully into a smaller scale version: the aramanthus still drape richly down the side of the cake and the twigs reach up from the midst of the arrangement of warm red, orange and gold flowers at the base. The cupcakes are a decadent display of large flowers crammed onto bright-orange-cased little cakes.

BOUNTIFUL BERRIES

Celebrate the plenty that autumn has to offer, with this design of juicy-looking raspberries, blackberries and soft flowers, all set against a strong dark background. In the garden the hydrangea heads may be turning brown, but here we can keep them fresh in pale green and pile them up with ranunculus, scabious pods, dahlias and delicate ferns.

You will need

CAKE

- Top tier: 10cm (4in) round cake, 7.5cm (3in) high
- Middle tier: 15cm (6in) round cake, 15cm (6in) high
- Bottom tier: 25cm (10in) round cake, 10cm (4in) high

BUTTERCREAM

- 800g–1kg (1lb 12oz–2lb 4oz) dark brown (Sugarflair Dark Brown)
- 200g (7oz) two-tone light and medium caramel (Sugarflair Caramel)
- 300g (10½oz) dark green (Sugarflair Spruce Green + hint of Brown)
- 300g (10½oz) light green (Sugarflair Gooseberry)
- 500g (1lb 2oz) two-tone green (Sugarflair Gooseberry + hint of Brown)
- 500g (1lb 2oz) light peach (Sugarflair Super White + hint of Peach + hint of Brown)
- 400g (14oz) very light pink (Sugarflair Super White + hint of Pink + hint of Brown)
- 50g (1¾oz) dark yellow (Sugarflair Melon + hint of Autumn)
- 200g (7oz) dark violet (Sugarflair Grape Violet + Black)
- 200g (7oz) dark red (Sugarflair Grape Claret + Red)
- 500g (1lb 2oz) two-tone light green and white (Sugarflair Gooseberry and Super White)
- 100g (3½oz) white (Sugarflair Super White)
- 500–600g (1lb 2oz–1lb 5oz) extra plain buttercream for blobs

EQUIPMENT

- Wilton petal nozzle 104
- Wilton petal nozzle 102
- Wilton petal nozzle 101
- Wilton star nozzle 13
- Wilton leaf nozzle 352
- Wilton leaf nozzle 65s
- Piping bags
- Parchment paper/baking sheet
- Board or cookie tray
- Scissors

1. Pipe the ranunculus, scabious pods, raspberries, blackberries and round leaves in advance: use light green (centres) and light peach (outer petals) buttercream for the ranunculus, two-tone green (see Buttercream Basics, Piping) for the scabious pods, dark red for the raspberries, dark violet for the blackberries and light green for the pointed leaves (see Piping Flowers). Set them aside.

2. Pipe some ferns directly onto the cake, using Wilton leaf nozzle 65s with light caramel buttercream (see Piping Flowers). Add a small shell border in dark caramel to make the central stem of each fern.

3. Pipe a small thin blob of plain buttercream in each position you wish to place the pre-piped pointed leaves, and then attach them to the cake.

4. Pipe a mound of buttercream for each hydrangea, then pipe them directly onto the surface of the cake using a Wilton petal nozzle 102 and two-tone light green and white buttercream (see Piping Flowers). You can pre-pipe them in advance if you prefer.

4

5. Pipe more blobs ready to evenly position the remaining flowers and add some of the raspberries and blackberries.

6. Arrange the scabious pods and ranunculus on the buttercream blobs and make sure you leave space for the dahlia.

7. Place the remaining berries in between the other flowers.

8. Pipe the dahlia directly on the cake using a Wilton leaf nozzle 352 with very light pink buttercream and give it a dark yellow centre (see Piping Flowers).

TIP

The space between the bottom and middle tier is quite wide, so to avoid having to use really large blobs of buttercream, you can bake extra cupcakes or use the cake trimmings to make into cakepops mixture to create the mounds to elevate the flowers.

For the cakepops mixture use one part cake crumbs to a half part buttercream, then mash together.

9. Pipe leaves to fill any gaps using a Wilton leaf nozzle 352 with light green buttercream.

10. Add baby's breath to cover the remaining gaps using a Wilton star nozzle 13 with white buttercream. Make sure you pipe these flowers in little clusters as shown.

9

10

Bountiful Berries One-tier and Cupcakes

We've created a simple round single-tier cake and piled its top with all the lovely flowers and berries from its bigger sibling. Because we are the 'Buttercream Queens' we've naturally made everything with buttercream, but with this design you could choose to cover your cake in milk or dark chocolate, and even pipe the ferns in melted white chocolate. We'll forgive you! Just make the cupcakes in brown cases to match the dark brown of the main cake, and top them with plenty of berries and flowers.

RED AND GOLD FALL FOLIAGE

Bold, bright and full of autumn colour, this cake evokes the brilliant display of
red, orange and yellow leaves produced by the forests of New England in the fall.
Maple leaves and acorns cluster with fiery marigolds and freesia at the corners, and
the middle tier is sprayed with decadent metallic edible colour to add sparkle.

You will need

CAKE

- Top tier: 10cm (4in) square cake, 7.5cm (3in) high

- Middle tier: 15cm (6in) square cake, 10cm (4in) high

- Bottom tier: 20cm (8in) square cake, 15cm (6in) high

BUTTERCREAM

- 800g–1kg (1lb 12oz–2lb 4oz) dark red (Sugarflair Red Extra + hint of Dark Brown)

- 600g (1lb 5oz) red-orange (Sugarflair Tangerine + Red)

- 600g (1lb 5oz) orange (Sugarflair Tangerine + hint of Red)

- 400g (14oz) orange (Sugarflair Tangerine + hint of Autumn Leaf)

- 50g (1¾oz) yellow (Sugarflair Autumn Leaf)

- 50g (1¾oz) green (Sugarflair Gooseberry + hint of White)

- 250g (9oz) light orange (Sugarflair Tangerine + hint of Red)

- 250g (9oz) dark orange (Sugarflair Tangerine + hint of Red)

- 200g (7oz) light caramel (Sugarflair Caramel)

- 300g (10½oz) brown (Sugarflair Dark Brown)

- 500–600g (1lb 2oz–1lb 5oz) extra plain buttercream for blobs

EQUIPMENT

- Wilton petal nozzle 103

- Wilton petal nozzle 102

- Wilton star nozzle 13

- Maple leaf template (see Templates)

- Angled palette knife

- Airbrush machine

- Gold or bronze airbrush colour

- Piping bags

- Parchment paper

- Board or cookie tray

- Cake Cloth

- Cake scraper

- Toothpick (cocktail stick)

1. To make the maple leaves in advance, place a small piece of parchment paper on top of your maple leaf template (see Templates). Use light or dark orange buttercream and hold the piping bag with the opening of a Wilton petal nozzle 103 straight onto the surface, at a 90 degree angle to it. Continuously squeeze as you go back and forth on one side of a leaf section.

2. Carry on with the other side of the leaf section, then complete the rest of the leaf. Pipe more leaves in light and dark orange and set them aside.

3. Pipe the marigolds and the 'nut' part of the acorns in advance: use red-orange and orange buttercream for the marigolds and brown for the body of the acorns (see Piping Flowers). Next, crumb coat the tiers (see Cake Basics) and then apply a thin layer of dark red buttercream onto your middle tier. Spread it evenly.

4. Using your angled palette knife, make a gentle tapping motion on the still-wet surface to create some peaks.

5. Airbrush the middle tier with gold or bronze airbrush colour.

6. Give the top and bottom tier a smooth covering of dark red buttercream, and stack the cakes (see Cake Basics).

7. Pipe a small blob or two of red buttercream onto the side of the cake where you want to position the maple leaves.

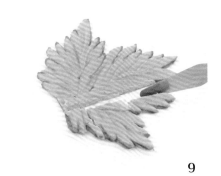

8. Gently stick your maple leaves to the surface of the cake.

9. Some of the maple leaves at the corners will have to be cut using a palette knife or a knife before being positioned on the cake.

10. Some of the maple leaves will be overlapping. If a leaf breaks, you can still use the pieces.

11. Pipe more blobs of buttercream then position the marigolds.

12. Pipe some freesia stems using green buttercream in a piping bag with a tiny hole at the tip (see Piping Flowers).

9

8

10

11

12

TIP

After covering the middle tier and creating the texture, let the cake settle for a few hours before airbrushing it. Fresh buttercream still has oil in the surface, but allowing it to set for a while will make the airbrushed colour work better.

The maple leaves are thin and can easily break so make sure you position and work with them as fast as you can. You can put them back in the freezer if they start to soften, or air-dry them overnight before freezing them to make them firmer to work with.

13. Pipe the freesias straight onto the cake using orange buttercream and giving them a yellow centre (see Piping Flowers).

14. Position the acorns and finish them off by piping a swirl of light caramel buttercream on top using a Wilton star nozzle 13.

15. Pipe the stem of the acorn using a slightly darker caramel buttercream (just add a tiny touch more colour to what's left of the light caramel buttercream) in a piping bag with a tiny hole cut at the tip.

TIP

Red is a very strong colour so if you are using it in any two-tone or blending technique with another colour, make sure that the blending colour is two or three shades lighter.

Red and Gold Fall Foliage One-tier and Cupcakes

The palette knife texture that we used on the middle tier of the main cake is again put to good use on the one-tier version of this glowing red autumn design. We find that it gives the rich red more depth, and you can further enhance the 'glow' with a light spray of gold or bronze edible paint. Add flowers and acorns to the top, and position your maple leaves so that they give the impression of a recent fall of leaves. The cupcakes look great in red-orange cases, and nothing looks cuter on top than a little cluster of acorns!

PERFECT PUMPKIN

Cause a stir with this amazing pumpkin – the perfect centrepiece for an autumnal celebration! The key to its realistic shape is in the carving of the cake, so pay careful attention to the instructions below. Once you have the round shape mastered, you can simply add a selection of gorgeous flowers and foliage to the top tier.

You will need

CAKE

- Top tier: 7.5–10cm (3–4in) round cake, 7.5cm (3in) high
- Bottom tier: 20cm (8in) round cake, 20cm (8in) high

BUTTERCREAM

- 700–800g (1lb 9oz–1lb 12oz) light caramel (Sugarflair White base + hint of Caramel)
- 200g (7oz) dark caramel (Sugarflair White base + hint of Caramel)
- 200g (7oz) light green (Sugarflair White base + hint of Gooseberry)
- 600g (1lb 5oz) light pink (Sugarflair White base + Dusky Pink + hint of Egyptian Orange)
- 300g (10½oz) light peach (Sugarflair White base + Egyptian Orange + hint of Dusky Pink)
- 250g (9oz) dark orange (Sugarflair Egyptian Orange + Autumn Leaf)
- 250g (9oz) light orange (Sugarflair Egyptian Orange + Autumn Leaf)

- 400g (14oz) mid orange (Sugarflair Autumn Leaf + Orange + hint of Red)
- 300g (10½oz) dark red (Sugarflair Burgundy + Brown)
- 200g (7oz) medium red (Sugarflair Burgundy + hint of Grape Violet)
- 150g (5½oz) dark green (Sugarflair Spruce Green)
- 150g (5½oz) dark purple (Sugarflair Grape Violet)
- 200g (7oz) very light pink (Sugarflair White base + hint of Claret)
- 300g (10½oz) light green (Sugarflair White base + hint of Gooseberry)
- 400g (14oz) dark green (Sugarflair Spruce Green + hint of White)
- 200g (7oz) dark blue (Sugarflair Navy Blue + hint of Baby Blue)
- 300g (10½oz) eucalyptus (Sugarflair Eucalyptus)
- 500–600g (1lb 2oz–1lb 5oz) extra plain buttercream for blobs

EQUIPMENT

- Wilton petal nozzle 124
- Wilton petal nozzle 104
- Wilton chrysanthemum nozzle 81
- Wilton leaf nozzle 352
- Cake card for template
- Serrated knife
- 30cm (12in) round cake board
- Small serrated knife
- Piping bags
- Parchment paper/baking sheet
- Board or cookie tray
- Scissors
- Toothpicks (cocktail sticks)
- Pen/pencil
- Piece of plastic/card scraper
- Cake Cloth
- Cake scraper
- Angled palette knife
- Narrow tip palette knife

1. Make the roses, kale, two sorts of photinia leaves and the thistle centres in advance: use light pink and a two-tone combination of light pink and light peach buttercream for the roses, very light pink (centres), light green (middle layers) and dark green (outer layers) for the kale, dark red and medium red for the red two-tone photinia leaves, dark green and dark purple for the remaining two-tone photinia leaves, and dark blue for the thistle centres (see Piping Flowers). Next, stack and fill the bottom cake tier, until you have a cake that is 20cm (8in) high (see Cake Basics). Freeze the cake for 1–2 hours (see Tip). Cut a 12.5–15cm (5–6in) circular template from cake card and place your guide centrally on top of your cake. Hold your knife at an angle and start trimming about 1.3cm (½in) off the corners of the top edge all the way around.

CARVING TIP

We find it very helpful when carving a cake if it is partially frozen, so that it doesn't crumble and fall apart when we work with it. Pop it in the freezer for an hour or two to achieve the right consistency. To avoid carving altogether, you can always use ball cake tins, or two stainless steel or pyrex bowls, but the carving technique will let you create any size or shape of cake you wish. If you are trying to achieve a really tall cake, you may also substitute the bottom cake sponge with a firmer medium, such as rice crispy cake or a cake dummy, to avoid the bottom layer being squashed by the weight of the cake above, and the filling being squeezed out at the sides. Another option is to dowel properly (see Cake Basics) and place a cake board between layers about halfway through the cake.

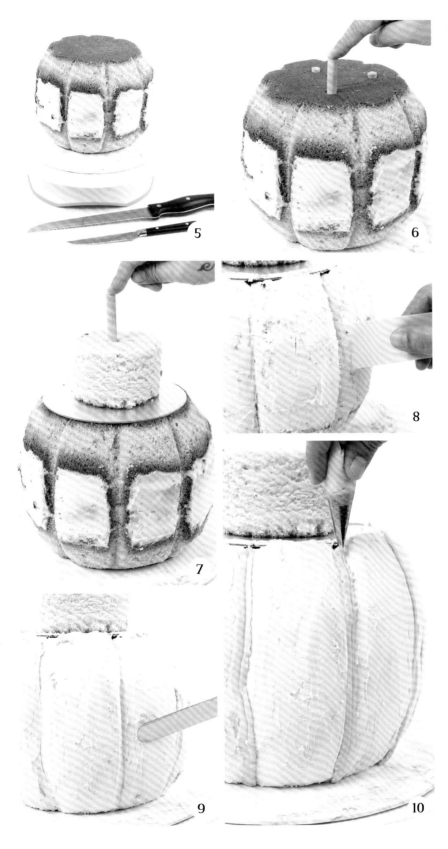

2. Place the cake board on top of the cake, slide your hand under and quickly flip the cake over.

3. Place the 12.5–15cm (5–6in) cake card template on top of the cake and repeat the same process. Keep carving the cake and carefully make it into a round shape.

4. Fold your round template in half four times until the folds in the circle make eight segments.

5. Use this guide to mark the ribs of the pumpkin and trim to make slightly deeper indentations and rounded corners. Use a small serrated knife to refine these details.

6. Cut three or four dowels to the height of your pumpkin and insert them (see Cake Basics).

7. Place the top tier cake on a 7.5–10cm (3–4in) cake board (to match the size of the top of your pumpkin), having made a hole in the centre of the board for a dowel to pass through. Cut a long central dowel and insert all the way down to the bottom of the cake (see Cake Basics).

8. Crumb coat your cake with light caramel buttercream (see Cake Basics). You can use a small piece of plastic scraper to even the buttercream out and to get into the ribs, then chill the cake in the fridge for 20–30 minutes or until firm.

9. Apply the final covering of light caramel buttercream, spreading it evenly (see Cake Basics). For shading, apply small blobs of dark caramel buttercream randomly and lightly spread them with an angled palette knife.

10. Apply very light green buttercream on the ribs of the pumpkin with a Wilton leaf nozzle 352 or just a plain piping bag.

11. Use a narrow tip palette knife to spread the very light green buttercream, but avoid spreading it too much as you will finish the job of blending it in the next step.

12. Use a small piece of plastic scraper to blend the colours to the background. Scrape from the centre of the rib outwards.

13. Use a small piece of Cake Cloth and lightly smooth the surface (see Cake Basics). Leave a little bit of rough texture all the way around to make the pumpkin look realistic.

14. Crumb coat the top tier with plain buttercream.

15. Pipe fresh blobs of plain buttercream to secure the flowers to the cake, then start adding them. Position your other floral elements, making sure you leave a space for the chrysanthemum flowers.

16. Pipe your chrysanthemums directly onto the cake with a Wilton petal nozzle 81, some in dark orange, some in mid orange and some in light orange buttercream (see Piping Flowers).

17. Pipe the leaves of the thistle flowers using eucalyptus buttercream and a Wilton leaf nozzle 352 nozzle, as shown, creating a spot for the thistle centre to go amongst the leaves.

18. Quickly place the centre of the thistle flower.

19. Pipe some more leaves to fill gaps, using dark green buttercream and a Wilton leaf nozzle 352.

20. Quickly position and insert the long pre-piped photinia leaves to finish the cake.

Perfect Pumpkin
One-tier and Cupcakes

This is just a smaller version of the main Perfect Pumpkin, so you'll still need to carve your cake to create the right shape, you'll just be starting with a 15cm (6in) cake, which might make things easier as a suitable sized half-sphere cake pan should be simple to source. And you won't need a top tier – we just topped the pumpkin with a stalk, created by pressure piping (see Piping Flowers), and positioned the flowers in a garland around it. We've added a second arrangement of flowers and foliage at the base of the cake. Top your cupcakes with a selection of the flowers, and use shortened photinia leaves so they don't get knocked off when the cupcake is picked up.

Winter

WINTER WARMER

Did you know that apples were once a common ornament for the Christmas tree? Here they decorate a cake that is all about some of the best elements of the winter season – bringing nature indoors and getting cosy! You can evoke the warmest of knitwear with the piped background patterns in this lovely design.

You will need

CAKE

- Top tier: 10cm (4in) round cake, 7.5cm (3in) high
- Middle tier: 15cm (6in) round cake, 10cm (4in) high
- Bottom tier: 20cm (8in) square cake, 7.5cm (3in) high

BUTTERCREAM

- 400–500g (14oz–1lb 2oz) light caramel (Sugarflair Caramel)
- 400–500g (14oz–1lb 2oz) light brown (Sugarflair Dark Brown)
- 700–800g (1lb 9oz–1lb 12oz) marbled light/dark brown (Sugarflair Dark Brown)
- 300g (10½oz) white (Sugarflair Super White)
- 100g (3½oz) dark yellow (Sugarflair Melon + hint of Autumn Leaf)
- 50g (1¾oz) light chestnut (Sugarflair Chestnut)
- 200g (7oz) light green (Sugarflair Gooseberry)
- 300g (10½oz) dark green (Sugarflair Spruce Green)
- 500–600g (1lb 2oz–1lb 5oz) yellow (Sugarflair Melon + hint of Autumn Leaf)
- 500–600g (1lb 2oz–1lb 5oz) red (Sugarflair Red Extra)
- 100g (3½oz) bright green (Sugarflair Bitter Lemon + hint of Gooseberry + hint of Melon)
- 200g (7oz) very light green (Sugarflair White + hint of Gooseberry)
- 500–600g (1lb 2oz–1lb 5oz) extra plain buttercream for blobs

EQUIPMENT

- Wilton petal nozzle 104
- Wilton star nozzle 363 or 21
- Wilton basketweave nozzle 47
- Wilton leaf nozzle 352
- Wilton round nozzle 10
- Wilton round nozzle 12 (optional)
- Piping bags
- Parchment paper/baking sheet
- Board or cookie tray
- Ruler
- Toothpick (cocktail stick)
- DinkyDoodle Shell & Shine
- Old paint brush
- Cake Cloth
- Cake scraper
- Angled palette knife
- Flat-tipped modelling tool

1. Pipe the apples and lemons in advance using red for the apples and yellow for the lemons, and spray both with DinkyDoodle Shell & Shine (see Piping Flowers). Set them aside.

2. Crumb coat and cover the top two cake tiers with light caramel buttercream, giving them a perfectly smooth surface (see Cake Basics). Cover the bottom tier in the same way using light brown buttercream. Mark the vertical lines for your knitted pattern on the top two cake tiers using a ruler and a toothpick (cocktail stick).

3. For the middle tier: use light caramel buttercream and pipe a 'shell' design by holding a Wilton star nozzle 363 (or a star nozzle 21) positioned to one side of the guide line with the opening touching the cake surface. Squeeze the piping bag until the buttercream fans out, then slowly lift the piping bag and pull it gently to the guide line as you release the pressure.

4. Repeat the process on the other side of the guide line to create a 'v' shape, then carry on all the way down the guide line.

5. Pipe small shell borders, using a piping bag with small hole at the tip, on both sides of the shell design. Repeat this vertical design on each of the guide lines all around the middle tier.

TIP

To evenly space the pattern lines, create a guide: wrap a strip of paper around the circumference of each tier, remove it and then keep folding the strip in half to give you the measurement of each panel. The folds should be approximately 2.5cm (1in) apart. Use them to guide where you make your vertical lines.

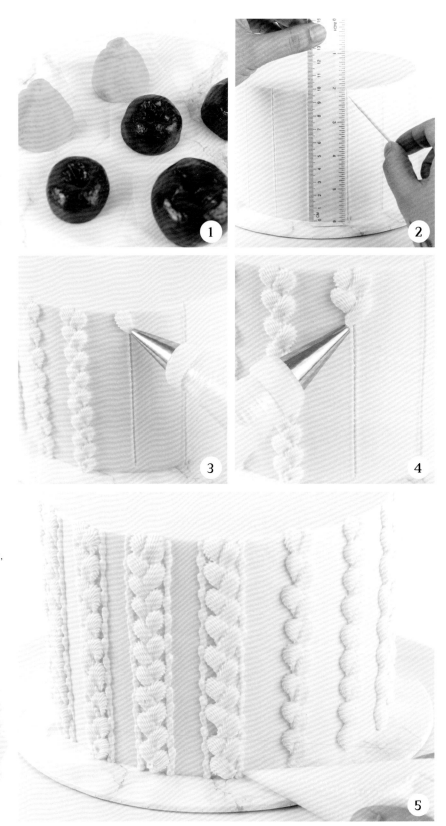

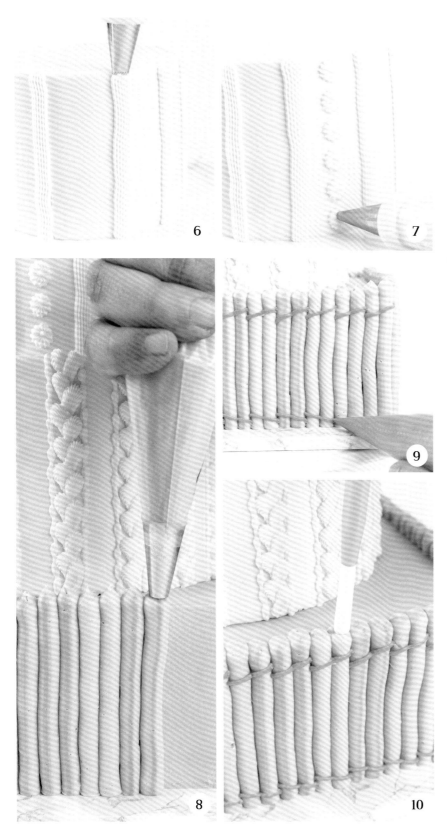

6. For the top tier: use light caramel buttercream and pipe lines using a Wilton basketweave nozzle 47 with the serrated side facing up. Make the first line just to the left of a guide line, being sure you cover the guide mark. Make a second line just to the right of the next guide line, then repeat this for the rest of the lines. In this way you will have alternating big and small spaces between pairs of piped lines.

7. Using the same Wilton star nozzle 363, pipe a vertical row of around five or six flat round 'buttons' with small spaces in between, in one of the wider spaces. Repeat in all the wider spaces around the top tier. After completing all decorations on the top and middle tier, stack all the cakes together (see Cake Basics).

8. Prepare your piping bag using marbled light and dark brown buttercream (see Buttercream Basics, Nozzles and Piping) and a Wilton round nozzle 10. Pipe the vertical 'twigs' all around the bottom cake tier with continuous pressure on the piping bag. Work from the bottom to the top edge for each twig, and create a slight protrusion at the top above the edge of the cake. Do not leave any gaps between the twigs.

9. Pipe 'stitches' on the top and bottom of the twigs using a piping bag with a tiny hole at the tip and chestnut buttercream. Pipe diagonal simple lines, grouping two twigs per stitch. Repeat the same process at the bottom of the twigs.

10. When the buttercream is crusted, use a flat-tipped modelling tool to flatten the end of each twig. You could just use your fingers if you do not have this tool.

11. Pipe guide marks, then pipe the pine leaves using a piping bag with a small hole at the tip and dark green buttercream (see Piping Flowers).

12. Pipe two-tone leaves using a Wilton leaf nozzle 352 with bright and dark green buttercream.

13. Pipe some blobs of plain buttercream and position the apples. Elevate some of them to give nice depth to the arrangements.

14. Repeat the same process to position the lemons.

15. Pipe more blobs for the magnolias and poinsettias.

16. Now that you have determined where the magnolias and poinsettias will go, you can pipe more of both sorts of leaves between them before you pipe the flowers.

17. Pipe the poinsettias directly onto the cake using a Wilton leaf nozzle 352 with two-tone white and light green buttercream (see Buttercream Basics, Piping), giving them yellow centres (see Piping Flowers).

18. Pipe the magnolias onto the cake using a Wilton petal nozzle 104 with white buttercream, and give them light green and yellow centres (see Piping Flowers).

Winter Warmer
One-tier and Cupcakes

Let your buttercream knitting shine through in this simplified version of this cosy winter cake! Just combine both of the vertical piped patterns on a single tier, and add an arrangement of flowers and fruit on the top and at the base. The top arrangement is a curving semi-circle that frames one side of the cake's top surface. Keep your cupcakes looking fresh and clean with white paper cases that fit the wintry theme.

DEAR REINDEER

Out of a halo of flowers and foliage a deer peeps – on his noble head a crown
of lilies and pine cones, and above that a set of impressive antlers. This
may look like a design that would challenge your artistic abilities, but
never fear, the line drawing is achieved by tracing a template. Simple!

You will need

CAKE

- Top tier: 10cm (4in) round cake, 7.5cm (3in) high
- Middle tier: 15cm (6in) round cake, 10cm (4in) high
- Bottom tier: 20cm (8in) round cake, 10cm (4in) high

BUTTERCREAM

- 1.5kg (3lb 5oz) white (Sugarflair Super White)
- 200g (7oz) light violet (Sugarflair White base + Grape Violet + hint of Brown)
- 200g (7oz) medium violet (Sugarflair White base + Grape Violet + hint of Brown)
- 200g (7oz) light yellow (Sugarflair White base + hint of Autumn Leaf)
- 300g (10½oz) light blue (Sugarflair White base + hint of Baby Blue + hint of Navy Blue)
- 50g (1¾oz) very light blue (Sugarflair White base + hint of Baby Blue)
- 400g (14oz) dark green (Sugarflair Spruce Green)
- 400g (14oz) light green (Sugarflair White base + hint of Spruce Green)
- 400g (14oz) brown (Sugarflair Dark Brown)
- 500g (1lb 2oz) light caramel (Sugarflair White base + hint of Caramel)
- 100–200g (3½–7oz) light eucalyptus (Sugarflair Eucalyptus + hint of Black)
- 50g (1¾oz) black (Sugarflair Black)
- 500–600g (1lb 2oz–1lb 5oz) extra plain buttercream for blobs

EQUIPMENT

- Wilton petal nozzle 104
- Wilton petal nozzle 103
- Wilton petal nozzle 102
- Wilton petal nozzle 97L
- Wilton leaf nozzle 65s
- Wilton leaf nozzle 352
- Antler and deer templates (see Templates)
- Piping bags
- Parchment paper
- Board or cookie tray
- Scissors
- Pen/pencil
- Piece of paper/card
- Cake Cloth
- Cake scraper
- Angled palette knife
- Brown Wilton Candy Melts or any milk chocolate

1. Make the pine cones, calla lilies, round leaves and closed peonies in advance (see Piping Flowers): use brown buttercream for the pine cones, white for the calla lilies, dark green for the round leaves and light caramel for the closed peonies. Set them aside.

2. Place a piece of parchment paper over your antler pattern (see Templates). Melt pieces of chocolate or use Candy Melts and fill a piping bag without a nozzle. Cut a small hole at the tip and trace over the template. Let the chocolate harden.

3. Place a piece of parchment paper over your deer pattern (see Templates) and trace over with black buttercream in a piping bag with a very small hole at the tip.

4. Cover and stack your cakes, giving them a smooth covering of white buttercream (see Cake Basics). Position your deer pattern on the middle tier.

5. Lightly rub and trace over the pattern with your finger.

6. Carefully peel the parchment paper away.

7. Trace over any missing details and define the eyes and nose with black buttercream in a piping bag with a very small hole at the tip.

TIP

We have included a template for the picture of the deer that we used, but feel free to use other designs or patterns. You can search for 'printables' or 'how to draw...' on the internet and just look for the kind of design you have in mind. Before you print out your chosen image, flip the image vertically to avoid making a mirror image when you trace over it.

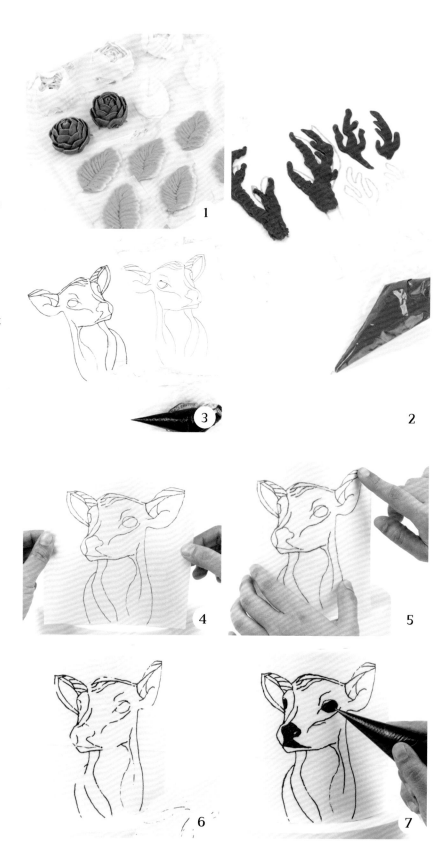

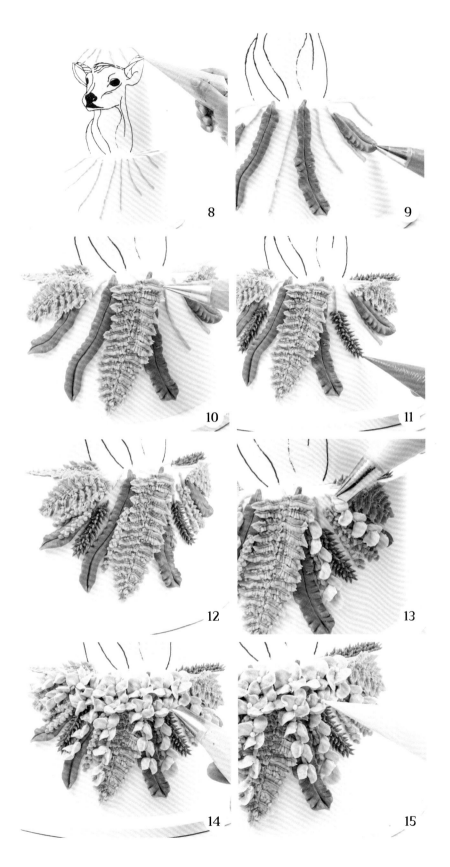

8. Use light green buttercream and pipe guide marks for the foliage.

9. Use Wilton leaf nozzle 352 with dark green buttercream to pipe long leaves. Continuously squeeze the piping bag as you drag it according to the length that you desire.

10. Pipe ferns using Wilton leaf nozzle 65s and light green buttercream (see Piping Flowers, Leaves).

11. Pipe spiky pine leaves using dark green buttercream in a piping bag with a small hole at the tip (see Piping Flowers, Leaves).

12. Pipe lavender flowers using alternating buds of light and medium violet in a piping bag with a small hole at the tip.

13. Pipe eucalyptus leaves with the simple petal technique (see Piping Flowers) using a Wilton petal nozzle 103 and light eucalyptus buttercream.

14. Pipe delphinium flowers using the simple petal technique again, with a Wilton petal nozzle 102 and light blue buttercream (see Piping Flowers).

15. Complete the delphiniums by piping dots using very light blue buttercream in a piping bag with a small hole at the tip.

16. Pipe fresh blobs of plain buttercream and position your pine cones.

17. Repeat the same process to position your peonies and calla lilies.

18. Quickly insert the chocolate antlers so they don't melt in your fingers.

19. Position and insert your pre-piped round leaves.

20. Fill any gaps with pulled-petal-type leaves (see Piping Flowers, Leaves) using Wilton leaf nozzle 352 and dark green buttercream.

21. Pipe the centres of the calla lily flowers using light yellow buttercream in a piping bag with a medium hole at the tip. Steadily squeeze the piping bag as you slowly pull until you reach the desired length, then release the pressure.

Dear Reindeer One-tier and Cupcakes

Using the tracing technique described in the instructions for the main reindeer cake, you can transfer a design onto the flat surface of the top of a single-tier square cake, as we have done here. In fact you might find this a little easier if it's your first go at this technique. We really like the way the chocolate antlers protrude above the cake in the bigger version, so we've carried that through to the smaller cake too. Make two floral arrangements, one on the head of the deer and one cascading over the cake side and framing the deer's neck. We couldn't resist adding little antlers to the cupcakes – they are sure to put a smile on anyone's face!

SHIMMERING WINTER WONDER

The delicate frosted surfaces of this cake will catch the pale winter light, making it shimmer. Clustering white roses and carnations are set off with delicate grey berries, pale leaves and frothy white blossoms. Every element should receive a pearl coating, but go carefully when airbrushing the wafer paper leaves.

You will need

CAKE

- Top tier: 15cm (6in) round cake, 10cm (4in) high
- Bottom tier: 20cm (8in) round cake, 20cm (8in) high

BUTTERCREAM

- 700g (1lb 9oz) light grey (Sugarflair Black)
- 1kg (2lb 4oz) white (Sugarflair Super White
- 100–200g (3½–7oz) light green (Sugarflair Gooseberry + hint of Brown)
- 100–200g (3½–7oz) eucalyptus (Sugarflair Eucalyptus + hint of Black)
- 100g (3½oz) grey (Sugarflair Black + hint of Eucalyptus)
- 250g (9oz) light green (Sugarflair Gooseberry + hint of Brown + White)

EQUIPMENT

- Wilton petal nozzle 104
- Wilton petal nozzle 103
- Wilton leaf nozzle 352
- Wilton writing nozzle 2 (optional)
- Dusty Miller (senico) template (see Templates)
- Green printed wafer paper
- Pen/pencil
- Scissors
- Angled palette knife
- Cake scraper
- Cake Cloth
- Piece of card
- Airbrush machine
- DinkyDoodle pearl airbrush colour
- Piping bags
- Parchment paper
- Board or cookie tray
- Tweezers

1. Cut 20–25 Dusty Miller (senecio) leaves (see Templates) from the green printed wafer paper and place them in a re-sealable bag.

2. Crumb coat then cover the bottom tier with light grey buttercream using the palette knife, smooth with the Cake Cloth and leave for 5–10 minutes to crust (see Buttercream Basics). Using a piece of card, hold it vertically and press the edge into the cake surface. You can also slightly bend the card to make a curved line. Repeat the process to give the bottom tier a lovely texture all the way around.

3. Cover the top tier with white buttercream and stack the cakes together (see Buttercream Basics). Airbrush the whole of the cake with pearl airbrush colour, and repeat with several coatings for the shine to show.

4. Make the brunia berries, using grey buttercream in a plain piping bag with a medium hole at the tip, by squeezing ball-shaped blobs on a board. You can choose to line the board with parchment paper to prevent sticking.

TIP

If you are not able to get the wafer paper printed in your desired colour, you can instead airbrush it using sage green colour. Make sure that the airbrushing nozzle is not too close to the wafer paper to prevent it from becoming soggy.

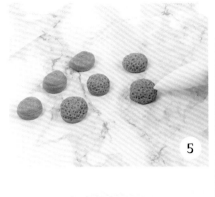

5

6

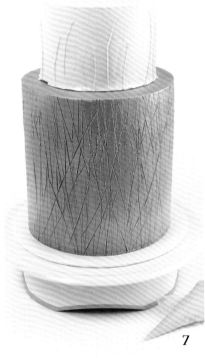

7

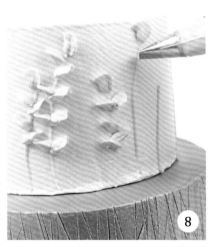

8

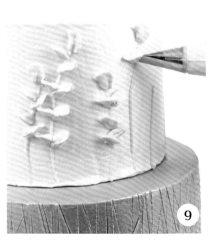

9

10

5. Leave the berries to crust for 5–10 minutes, then use a toothpick or a modelling tool to add a dotted texture by gently poking their surface.

6. Pipe the roses using petal nozzle 104 (see Piping Flowers) and the carnations by piping rings of ruffle petals with petal nozzle 103 (see Piping Flowers) onto parchment paper. Transfer onto a board or cookie tray, then airbrush flowers and brunia berries with pearl colour. Place in the freezer for about 10–15 minutes before arranging onto the cake.

7. Using your light green buttercream in a plain piping bag with a small hole at the tip, pipe some short stems on the side of the top cake tier.

8. Pipe the eucalyptus leaves by positioning the wide end of the petal nozzle 103 on the stem with the opening just slightly above the surface.

9. To make a leaf, gradually squeeze the piping bag while you slowly turn your hand towards the stem. Do not lift your hand away from the cake. Repeat the process to add leaves to all the stems you piped. Some leaves should be opposite each other, while others are alternating.

10. Determine the placement of your flowers and berries and make sure you pipe a fresh blob of buttercream on the cake surface first, ready to stick each one on.

11. Place the roses first, then the rest of the flowers. Secure them to the blob by using a couple of toothpicks (cocktail sticks) and poking the flowers on both ends as you slightly twist while pushing down.

12. Position the brunia berries in between the other flowers.

13. Use the leaf nozzle 352 to pipe some leaves (see Piping Flowers, Leaves).

14. Using white buttercream in a plain piping bag with a small hole at the tip, or using a writing nozzle 2, pipe clusters of small dots in areas that need a little more cover, so that you do not have to fill all the gaps full of leaves. These delicate white dots will look like baby's breath flowers.

15. Insert the wafer paper leaves. You can use tweezers to carefully push them to prevent breakage.

16. Touch up the pearl airbrushing again to give more shine to the leaves, berries and white filler flowers.

Winter Wonder One-tier and Cupcakes

For the smaller version of the shimmering winter cake, we continued the texture all over instead of just on the sides. The edges of each indented line will catch the light once the surface has been sprayed with pearl colouring. Follow the instructions from the main cake for creating the textured surface and piping the flowers. Just arrange the floral elements in a wreath on top of the one-tier cake and add a simple bead border around the base in silver to enhance the winter feel.

Use silver cupcake cases to create a glittering icy look, and add a selection of flowers, berries and leaves to complete your matching cupcakes.

FLORAL CHRISTMAS TREE

If you're looking for a Christmas cake with the wow factor, look no further! The sheer height of this towering tree gives it great impact, and it's bursting with gorgeous red, white and green flowers and foliage, which will fit perfectly with a traditional festive colour scheme.

You will need

CAKE

- Bottom tier: 15cm (6in) round cake, 10cm (4in) high
- Tree tier: two 20cm (8in) round cakes, 7.5cm (3in) high, and two 15cm (6in) round cakes, 7.5cm (3in) high

BUTTERCREAM

- 500g (1lb 2oz) red (Sugarflair Red Extra + hint of Brown)
- 400g (14oz) very light green (plain buttercream + Sugarflair Gooseberry)
- 500-600g (1lb 2oz-1lb 5oz) red (Sugarflair Red Extra)
- 400g (14oz) white (Sugarflair Super White)
- 400g (14oz) brown (Sugarflair Dark Brown)
- 50g (1¾oz) dark yellow (Sugarflair Melon + hint of Autumn Leaf)
- 500-600g (1lb 2oz-1lb 5oz) dark green (Sugarflair Spruce Green)
- 500-600g (1lb 2oz-1lb 5oz) medium green (Sugarflair Gooseberry + Spruce Green)
- 500-600g (1lb 2oz-1lb 5oz) light green (Sugarflair Gooseberry)
- 400-500g (14oz-1lb 2oz) extra plain buttercream for blobs and crumb coating

EQUIPMENT

- Wilton petal nozzle 103
- Wilton petal nozzle 102
- Wilton petal nozzle 124
- Wilton leaf nozzle 74
- Wilton leaf nozzle 352
- Wilton round nozzle 8
- Piping bags
- Parchment paper/baking sheet
- Board or cookie tray
- Scissors
- Piece of paper/card
- Cake Cloth
- Cake scraper
- Angled palette knife
- Dowel

1. Make the roses in advance using red and very light green buttercream (see Piping Flowers), then set them aside. Cover the 'pot' (the bottom tier) with chestnut buttercream and use a straight edge scraper to even it out (see Cake Basics).

2. Pipe small blobs of brown buttercream here and there around the cake sides, then spread them with an angled palette knife with a random motion.

3. Pipe random blobs of white buttercream and again spread them with the angled palette knife.

4. Use a scraper to scrape the sides in short strokes until whole cake has blended/marbled look.

5. Fill and stack the cakes together, and give the 'tree' (the top tier) a crumb coat of plain buttercream. Make sure to insert a central dowel that is as tall as the cake (see Cake Basics).

6. Mark the position of your very light green roses all around your cake with a guide mark, then pipe blobs with a little plain buttercream in the marks to attach the roses.

TIP

Follow the steps in Cake Basics for stacking and dowelling tall cakes, and see the tip for carving cakes in the Perfect Pumpkin project to help you shape your Christmas tree. The 'pot' can be a cake dummy that you permanently stick to the main board to give your tall cake added support.

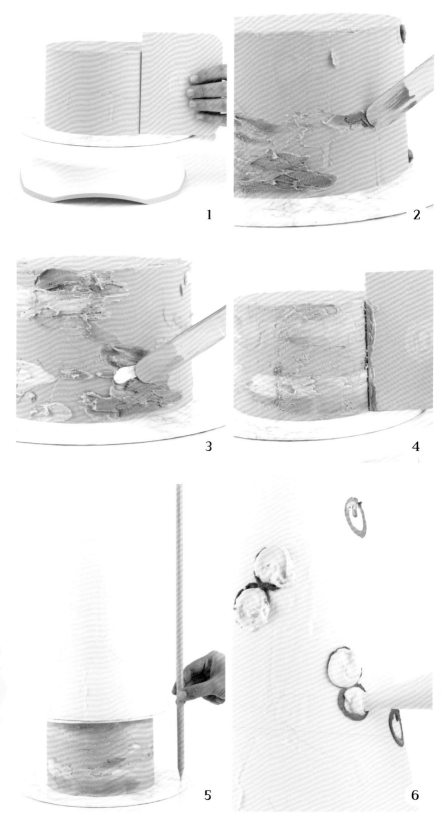

7. Place and secure the roses on the blobs.

8. Decide where you will position the other flowers and pipe more small blobs of buttercream. You can use letters or any symbols to remind you which blobs are for the poinsettias and which are for the cotton flowers.

9. Pipe egg-shaped blobs of brown buttercream where you will pipe your pine cones.

10. Pipe ruffle leaves using a Wilton leaf nozzle 74 and three different shades of green buttercream: light, medium and dark green.

11. Pipe the spikes of the pine cones on the brown blobs using a Wilton petal nozzle 102 with light brown buttercream (see Piping Flowers).

TIP

You can pipe the pine cones directly onto the cake or you can pre-pipe them. If you choose to make them in advance, you can freeze them, then cut them in half using a thin palette knife before applying them to the cake.

Make sure you prepare enough shades of green tinted buttercream to cover your entire cake. It's tricky to re-create exactly the same shade if you run out.

12. Pipe the cotton flowers with a Wilton round nozzle 8, directly onto the cake, with their details added with brown buttercream and a piping bag with a small hole at the tip (see Piping Flowers).

13. Pipe the poinsettia using a Wilton leaf nozzle 352 with red buttercream, and add the centres in dark yellow (see Piping Flowers).

14. Pipe pulled flowers using a Wilton petal nozzle 102 and red buttercream, then give them light green centres (see Piped Flowers).

15. Pipe red berries using a piping bag with a small hole at the end.

16. Pipe some more buttercream blobs on the very top of the cake and position the red roses.

17. Pipe some leaves around the red roses using a Wilton leaf nozzle 352 and dark green buttercream to cover the blobs (see Piping Flowers).

Floral Christmas Tree One-tier and Cupcakes

The single-tier version of this elaborate cake is a dome of festive flowers – red, white and green, like the tree. Use a half-sphere ball cake pan, or carve a round cake to make the underlying shape. You can boost the dome shape on the top with a mound of buttercream beneath your roses, cotton flowers, poinsettia, pine cones and other elements. The cupcakes continue the traditional colour scheme and look great in bright green cases.

TEMPLATES

All templates are shown at 100%. Downloadable versions are available from: http://ideas.sewandso.co.uk/patterns.

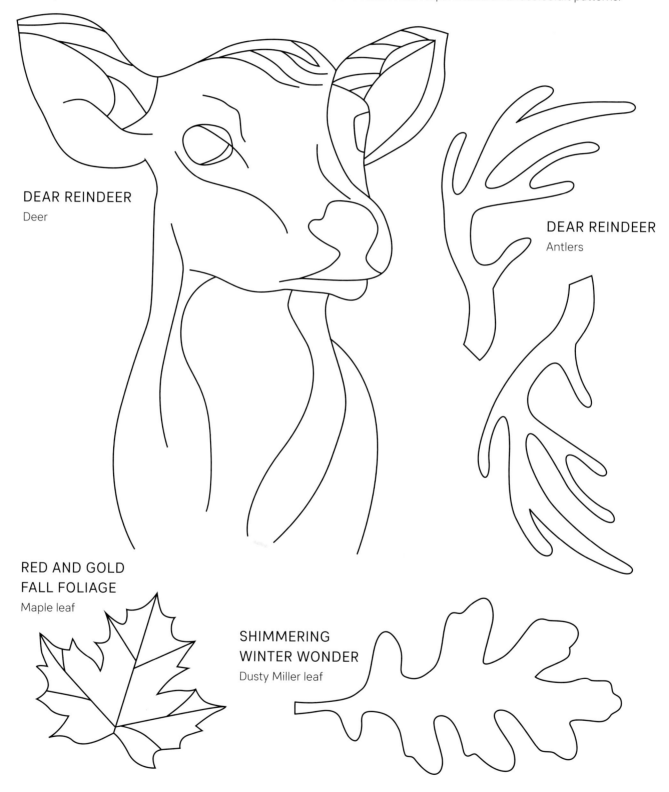

DEAR REINDEER
Deer

DEAR REINDEER
Antlers

**RED AND GOLD
FALL FOLIAGE**
Maple leaf

**SHIMMERING
WINTER WONDER**
Dusty Miller leaf

SUPPLIERS

UK SUPPLIERS

QUEEN OF HEARTS COUTURE CAKES

23 Jersey Road, Hanwell,
London W7 2JF
+44 (0)1634 235407 / 075813 95801
www.queenofheartscouturecakes.com
*Supplier of food colouring pastes
and cake decorating materials*

WILTON UK

Merlin Park, Wood Lane, Erdington,
Birmingham B24 9QI
0121 386 3200
www.wilton.co.uk
*Big selection of nozzles and
cake decorating supplies*

DINKYDOODLE DESIGNS

Private Road No. 8, Colwick,
Nottingham NG4 2JX
+44 (0)203 4788625
www.dinkydoodledesign.co.uk
*Supplier of airbrush machines
and colours*

THE CAKE DECORATING COMPANY

1st Floor Tickled Trout Services,
Junction 31 M6, Preston New Road,
Samlesbury PR5 0UJ
+44 (0)115 969 9800
www.thecakedecoratingcompany.co.uk
*Range of cake decorating materials
and edible printing*

US SUPPLIER

THE WILTON STORE

7511 Lemont Road,
Darien IL 60561
+1 630-985-6000
www.wilton.com
*Big selection of nozzles and
cake decorating supplies*

ABOUT THE AUTHORS

Best friends Valeri Valeriano and Christina Ong had their eureka moment in buttercream decorating in 2011, in a small kitchen equipped with an oven the size of a toaster. With knowledge gleaned from a YouTube tutorial and armed only with a zip lock bag, they discovered a hidden talent and a passion so vibrant that it has taken their lives in an entirely new direction – and all over the world.

The Queens of Buttercream developed techniques such as lace design, crochet effect, palette knife painting and, of course, flower piping, with which they elevated buttercream decoration to a whole new level. They now teach classes throughout Europe, the United States, Asia, the Middle East and Australia. With their success, the duo has vowed to spread their buttercream knowledge in the indefatigable manner with which they do everything else. As they share their recipes, techniques, tips and secrets they continuously innovate in order to deliver the very best to their students, readers and clients. Featured in popular magazines and television shows in the UK and internationally, they have also showcased their talents in three previous bestselling books, *The Contemporary Buttercream Bible* (2014), *100 Buttercream Flowers* (2015), and *Buttercream One-tier Wonders* (2016), all translated and offered in many languages.

To find out more visit www.queenofheartscouturecakes.com or www.facebook.com/QueenofHeartsCoutureCakes or follow Valeri and Christina on Twitter at @queenofheartscc

ACKNOWLEDGMENTS

When we started shifting from our day job to our cake journey, we had the mind-set that we would always make big plans, aim high in work and hope that our passion would move us beyond our plans and dreams. It was never easy, but because of the people who believed in us and supported us, we are who we are now.

We are forever grateful and indebted to our F+W media family. You are the team that inspires us to make extraordinary projects. Ame Verso, thank you for always challenging us to do so much more than we can think of. Jeni Hennah and Anna Wade, thank you for making sure that all the pages will be nothing short of perfection. Jane Trollope, thank you for filling us with words when we can't think of any. Jason Jenkins, you are a rockstar! It's always fun working with you, taking beautiful photos.

To our Cake International family, right from the start you trusted us, you believed in what we can do and what we can give to people, we will be forever thankful.

To our friends in Wilton, you deliver the most awesome products and we will always be honoured to be part of your ever growing family. Thank you for always supporting us with our projects.

To our expanding number of friends and followers all over the world, thank you for trusting us. Sharing our knowledge with you makes us believe that we are doing something right in our lives.

Sam and Khushi, what a wonderful blessing you are to us. Dawn and Debbie, thank you for always supporting us and for being our inspirations.

To our forever proud families in the Philippines, we love you so much. Thank you for being the best fan group ever. Once again, this is for you.

GO #TEAMBUTTERCREAM

INDEX

A SEWANDSO BOOK

© F&W Media International, Ltd 2018

SewandSo is an imprint of F&W Media International, Ltd
Pynes Hill Court, Pynes Hill, Exeter, EX2 5AZ, UK

F&W Media International, Ltd is a subsidiary of F+W Media, Inc
10151 Carver Road, Suite #200, Blue Ash, OH 45242, USA

Text and Designs © Valeri Valeriano and Christina Ong 2018
Layout and Photography © F&W Media International, Ltd 2018

First published in the UK and USA in 2018

Valeri Valeriano and Christina Ong have asserted their right to be identified as authors
of this work in accordance with the Copyright, Designs and Patents Act, 1988.

A catalogue record for this book is available from the British Library.

ISBN-13: 978-1-4463-0664-2 paperback
SRN: R6805 paperback

ISBN-13: 978-1-4463-7571-6 PDF
SRN: R5390 PDF

ISBN-13: 978-1-4463-7572-3 EPUB
SRN: R5391 EPUB

Printed in China by RR Donnelley for:
F&W Media International, Ltd
Pynes Hill Court, Pynes Hill, Exeter, EX2 5AZ, UK

10 9 8 7 6 5 4 3 2 1

Content Director: Ame Verso
Managing Editor: Jeni Hennah
Project Editor: Jane Trollope
Proofreader: Cheryl Brown
Designer: Courtney Kyle
Photographer: Jason Jenkins
Production Manager: Beverley Richardson

F&W Media publishes high quality books on a wide range of subjects.
For more great book ideas visit: **www.sewandso.co.uk**

Layout of the digital edition of this book may vary depending on reader hardware and
display settings.